BEAT
VOICES

BEAT VOICES

EDITED BY

DAVID
KHERDIAN

AN ANTHOLOGY OF BEAT POETRY

HENRY HOLT
AND COMPANY
NEW YORK

Henry Holt and Company, Inc.
Publishers since 1866
115 West 18th Street
New York, New York 10011

Henry Holt is a registered
trademark of Henry Holt and Company, Inc.

Library of Congress Cataloging-in-Publication Data
Beat voices: an anthology of beat poetry / edited by David Kherdian.
    p.   cm.
Includes bibliographical references (p.).
    Summary: A collection of American poetry by and about the beat
generation, written by such poets as Gregory Corso, Jack Kerouac,
Diane di Prima, and Allen Ginsberg.
    1. Beat generation—Juvenile poetry.   2. American poetry—20th century.
3. Children's poetry, American.   [1. Beat generation—Poetry.   2. American
poetry—Collections.]   I. Kherdian, David.
PS614.B34 1995   811'.5408—dc20   94-36106

ISBN 0-8050-3315-7

First Edition—1995

Designed by Victoria Hartman

Printed in the United States of America
on acid-free paper.∞

10 9 8 7 6 5 4 3 2 1

To Paul Collinge and Mary Lyons

Contents

Introduction

How long has it been, I ask myself as I sit here staring out my window at a different landscape, three thousand miles from that place where I first met many of the poets in this collection. The year was 1960, the place San Francisco. I never dreamed then—nor I am sure did they—that their work would achieve the notoriety it has. But on reflection it is not surprising, for they were not only symbols of an age but authentic poets who had something urgent to say, and were willing to pay the price for their assaults on the status quo.

When I published my first book of poems—ten years to the month after my arrival in San Francisco—there was a receptive climate for poetry, even that of a beginning poet. The Beats had wrested poetry from the colleges and set it free. Suddenly the poems they were creating in an open form spoke to us as poetry had not done for a very long time. Their poetry was for us because it was energized by the changing needs of humanity itself. The Beats took us back to Walt Whitman and William Blake, and would carry us forward to the music of Bob Dylan, the Beatles, and all the new sounds of the New Age that were helping to spiritualize a culture that had been strangulated by its own materialism.

But I am getting ahead of myself. Since I was actively involved in the life of the 1960s, I would like to say something about my own background, giving the reader my take on the Movement at the point at which I entered the scene.

I arrived in San Francisco fresh out of college and lived there from January 1960 until the Hippie invasion of Haight-Ashbury. My one vivid and final remembrance of that time was riding with the novelist Richard Brautigan from North Beach to Haight-Ashbury, and his saying, as we approached the famous corner, "It's all a teenage slum now."

So the Beat Movement began for me in 1960, but by then the Movement—if it was ever a movement—had crested, and American youth had begun to move into a new period of social protest.

I arrived in North Beach still a naive Midwesterner, despite my twenty-eight years. I had been contained by the Army for two years and sheltered in college for four more, with my summer-long solitary tour of Europe my only break-through into the world at large.

The fifties! America had come a long way, and as far as it would ever go in the direction it was traveling. And it had arrived at nothing! If this was bliss, Hell would have been a welcome diversion. This is what everyone who was protesting was protesting against: the stagnant, stultifying, stupefying 1950s, with the buildup of the industrial-military complex, and America's paranoia over any form of self-expression that threatened the powers-that-be.

I was barely aware of Jack Kerouac's *On the Road* and Allen Ginsberg's *Howl*. I had read neither. I arrived in San Francisco completely unaware that America was changing, but certainly aware that a new energy was beginning to enter our lives. Where it had come from and where it was leading were the imponderables I hadn't yet begun to grasp.

With some of my hometown buddies (we had driven out

the day following my final college exam), I walked into the Anxious Asp off Grant Avenue and stepped into another world. I noticed first the hardwood, sawdust-covered floor, and then a voice coming from the corner, where a barefoot, long-haired young man sat playing a guitar and singing a folk song, with the people at the tables drinking espresso, all of them relaxed, at home with themselves and the place. Cool, laid-back, and alive!

This then was my place. And in that moment I knew that the life I had known was over, even though I did not know where this new way would take me. But I did know this: I would no longer have to scribble in secret. Here I would be one of many, and this alone would provide the freedom I required to be myself.

Down the block we found poetry and jazz at The Cellar, where I later heard Ray Charles (on the jukebox) for the first time. On Grant Avenue we found The Co-Existence Bagel Shop (a café), The Spaghetti Factory (a restaurant), and the Café Trieste, a coffee shop that was, and is still today, a popular hangout for writers.

Lawrence Ferlinghetti's City Lights Book Shop, America's first all-paperback bookstore, was a block or two away, and two doors down, at Discovery Bookshop, I met my first poet, David Meltzer, clerking where I too would clerk, and where I first went to find items for my William Saroyan collection. Even in 1960 Saroyan was the most famous writer living in the San Francisco Bay Area; and twenty years earlier he had been one of the most sought-after writers in America. But what he meant to me was something quite different from what he meant to other readers, and even other writers. Like myself, he was the offspring of Armenian immigrant parents, although he was of an earlier generation. For this reason his work had something to tell me about my lot as an Armenian-American. But even more important than this, he helped me to see, as a writer, that my material was as valid, as important, and as real as that of any other American writer. He impressed upon me, through his work, that an author did not need special material to be an outstanding writer. He just had to believe in the life he had been given, with the understanding that that very material could be the transformative stuff of literature—even great literature, as he had proven to me with his own work.

It was to meet Saroyan that I had come to California, for I was (again secretly) working on his bibliography, but I was too shy to either write to him or to call him when I arrived in the city.

And then an evening I will never forget. I was sitting at the bar at Tosca's, across from City Lights and Discovery; when I felt the door open behind me. I still hadn't turned around when the hairs on the back of my head stood up. To this day I do not know how I knew it was him, for I had never met him, and of course I hadn't even turned to look. He walked with his party to the back of the bar and took a table, where I could study him at my leisure. William Saroyan, who was for me America's greatest living writer!

After that we did meet, I completed my work on his bibliography, and we became friends. And then I was asked by a New York editor to compile checklists of the published writings of some of the poets of the San Francisco Renaissance. I took on the assignment at once, and decided almost as quickly that I would add personal portraits to the checklists, which would at last make me a published writer.

It wasn't long before I was living on Beaver Street, in the room vacated by Lew Welch, and sharing a kitchen with Phil

Whalen, who had the room next to mine. Allen Ginsberg and Peter Orlovsky were frequent visitors, as were Ron Loewinsohn, Richard Brautigan, Joanne Kyger, Gary Snyder, and Michael McClure, along with younger, aspiring poets who came to sit at the feet of the Master. The older poets (were they really affluent, or just generous, as I surmised?) brought food and even helped cook it, for Whalen was always broke, and he was always hungry, often standing in front of his nearly empty fridge (I almost always ate out), wondering where his next meal was coming from. Ginsberg, in a dedication years later, called Whalen a poet's poet, which explained the other poets' veneration, and of all the poets I sent my first book of poems to—long after when we had all scattered—he alone sent a response.

Kerouac's books were stored in the closet. Corso, the poet I most wanted to meet, was permanently gone (we would later meet at Dartmouth), but Lew Welch was still around, and we often drank together at Gino and Carlo's, where Jack Spicer held nightly court, and were I played pool with Don Carpenter, Ron Loewinsohn, and Richard Brautigan, among others, and where I would later meet Charles Olson, who told me what to expect at Northwestern, where I was headed to work on a Melville project.

By the time my book on the San Francisco poets was published, I had left San Francisco and was living in Fresno, where I had become Saroyan's sidekick and protégé. I was thirty-five and just married, and to my great surprise I was beginning to write poems. The only poem I had written before this time was composed at my last address in the Bay Area—I had extracted from the bottom of a letter I was writing to my sister what appeared to me to have the look and feel of verse. I typed it out on a clean sheet of paper and soon after showed it to David Meltzer, who encouraged me to send it to one of the local magazines. "It's good," he said simply. "Someone will take it." In Fresno, wandering around my backyard and then drifting inside, I began to write poem after poem, when poetry was the last thing I wanted to write. I wanted to write prose fiction, to become a dashing success like Saroyan, not a failed poet, for in America to be a poet was to be doomed to financial failure. I didn't yet know that I had no choice.

To support myself I taught the first course ever offered on the Beat poets at an American college, where I also worked as a consultant in special collections. And now I was a writer, although a very different kind of writer than I had once hoped to become. I soon left for New York, never to return, either to California or Wisconsin.

It is now thirty-four years later, and yet I feel fated to have compiled this anthology. My reasons are personal enough that I feel obliged to share them with you, the reader, whoever/wherever you are, for you will have your own reasons for picking up this book. I am aware that there has been a rise in popularity of the Beats, as well as a renewed interest in the 1960s. Why is that, I have asked myself, and how does it connect with what I felt in the Anxious Asp so long ago?

Periodically, it seems, a new interest in poetry awakens in a new generation, and nearly always this coincides with a revolution in poetry itself. The Beats heralded a revolution that didn't quite occur. And yet reverberations from that time remain. For years young people have had little access to our best poetry—poetry that is alive, that breathes, that touches our soul. To find it, they have had to turn to the last period when such poetry was being produced. The Beats go on singing to us because they once sang to themselves. That is what I recognized that first day in San Francisco. And whatever the song said then, it now says Hope, for this is what they had in abundance, and this is perhaps what their poems can provide for us today; along with faith in a better tomorrow, a tolerant day.

—*David Kherdian*
September 1994

After the Beat:
On to the Hippies

It is easy enough to say when the Beats began: it is all there in Allen Ginsberg's *Howl* (see page 3): the poet with his pals William Burroughs, Jack Kerouac, Gregory Corso, Peter Orlovsky, and Neal Cassady, in and around Columbia University, reading William Blake, Walt Whitman, William Carlos Williams, trying to live the mad/desperate lives of the nineteenth-century French poets Rimbaud and Baudelaire, hanging out with jazz musicians and hobos and criminals, seeing American history through the eyes of its victims—jailed and executed anarchists, lynched and segregated blacks, damned and hunted homosexuals—and sensing through all that yearning and darkness and striving for ecstasy that they knew some truth, some flash of revelation, that made the soothing hum of everyday life a horrible lie. That's how it started, but how did it end? With the Hippies.

Looking back to his days in San Francisco's North Beach, David Kherdian senses that a cosmic scene change had occurred when novelist Richard Brautigan realized that Haight-Ashbury had become a "teenage slum." The Hippies had replaced the Beats. Maybe, but that seems local and late. In a way, the Beats were gone by 1963, when President Kennedy was assassinated. Suddenly their alienation was popular. And two years later came a clear divide.

In the early sixties Bob Dylan wrote and recorded modern folk/protest songs. He sang about how "The Times They Are A-Changin'," and that the answer is "Blowin' in the Wind." Accompanied by acoustic guitar and solo harmonica, the songs were descendants of the union and labor songs, and tunes about hobos and migrant workers that Woody Guthrie composed during the Depression. Dylan played in clubs like Gerde's Folk City in New York and was only the most notable of a group of folk singers that included people like Rambling Jack Eliot and Joan Baez—when she sang Scottish ballads and Spanish songs.

Though he was not a Beat, Dylan had a lot in common with them. Inspired by Kerouac, he sang as the outsider to outsiders: he was the hobo, the voice of protest, the conscience addressing the nation from outside. The audience for the folk movement was an odd mix of the college kids who actually went to the clubs and bought the music and the oppressed peoples mentioned in the songs.

The Beats, too, were outsiders and liked it that way. They found more life and truth in other outsiders—junkies and jazz musicians, tramps and prisoners, mystical or tortured or Zen poets—than in the bland America of suburban lawns and network television. The media portrayed them wearing black shirts and pants, berets, often goatees on the men, leotards on the women. Even if the images were exaggerated, the Beats wanted to show that they were unlike the rest of the country, as unlike it as possible.

So they gathered in coffeehouses in odd locations: in Greenwich Village in New York City, which had a history of bohemian groups going back to the 1910s; in North Beach;

and anywhere "On the Road" that was out of sight, out of the mainstream. There they heard poetry and songs that gloried in the singers' isolation from a nation that had lost its soul; and there they proclaimed a new vision of Whitman's America.

The Beats had reason for their alienation. They grew up in a country that was racially segregated, that had little tolerance for public sexuality and none at all for attraction between people of the same sex. Many of them had been raised on stories of political and economic victims: the vilified singer Paul Robeson, the condemned anarchists Sacco and Vanzetti, the nearly lynched Scottsboro Boys, the executed spies Julius and Ethel Rosenberg. The America the Beats faced seemed to push everything they enjoyed, from jazz to poetry, as far to the margins as possible. No wonder they found their own home in those same margins.

In 1959, Ginsberg wrote what might have been a credo for the Beats:

> America is having a nervous breakdown. San Francisco is one of many places where a few individuals, poets, have had the luck and courage and fate to glimpse something new through the crack in mass consciousness; they have been exposed to some insight into their own nature, the nature of God.
>
> Therefore there has been great exaltation, despair, prophecy, strain, suicide, secrecy, and public gaiety among the poets of the city.
>
> Those of the general populace whose individual perception is sufficiently weak to be formed by stereotypes of mass communication disapprove and deny the insight. The police and newspapers have moved in, mad movie manufacturers from Hollywood are at this moment preparing bestial stereotypes of the scene.

See the contrast: the few individuals here and there versus "mass consciousness." Though he spoke of "great exaltation," "prophecy," and "public gaiety," Ginsberg's tone was dark. He began with a "nervous breakdown" and saw "strain, suicide, secrecy" along the way. Newspapers and movies were the purveyors of "stereotypes of mass communication." They were the enemies of divine "insight." All that would change for the Hippies.

In 1964 Dylan went to England and got a taste of the rising popularity of the Beatles. He began to experiment with the electric guitar and changed his look from a humble folk singer to a rock star. In the summer of 1965, at the Newport Folk Festival, he crossed the line: he "went electric." This was no mere change of instrument: it caused a great scandal and suggested a much larger shift for a whole generation.

Electric Dylan was not aimed at small groups in coffee-houses; he was on the forefront of the growing mass culture of rock. Hippies, who dressed in color-drenched tie-dye shirts, did not think of themselves as isolated from America but as the future of the nation. Timothy Leary suggested that everyone "turn on, tune in, drop out." That was an invitation to a mass transformation, not an individual protest. In *Howl* Ginsberg described the "best minds" of his generation as "destroyed by madness, starving, hysterical, naked." The Hippies called themselves the Woodstock Nation and looked forward happily to the rising of Atlantis, the coming of the age of Aquarius, or at the very least to joining with hundreds of thousands of their peers at rock concerts, be-ins, or mass protests. Ginsberg himself was photographed wearing beads and flowers and smiling beatifically at a "gathering of the tribes." He became an icon of the mass media, not its enemy.

Hippies joined rock bands and—however radical or mystical or ecstatic their songs—could hope for big record contracts and albums with spectacular psychedelic covers. Hippie songs and slogans and dress were soon absorbed into advertising campaigns for cars and cigarettes and airlines. Beats declaimed in coffeehouses and hoped, perhaps, that small out-of-the-way presses might print their words in very limited editions. Maynard G. Krebs in the popular TV show *Dobie Gillis* (played by Bob Denver, who went on to become Gilligan of *Gilligan's Island*) was the most visible Beat in the mass media, and he was a figure of fun, just as Ginsberg had warned. You could not sell anything by identifying with the Beats.

All of this matters now because the movements, in original as well as retro forms, are with us today. Deadheads play out Hippie dreams while coffee shops and goatees proliferate. But while both styles are out there to be imitated, the substance of the Beats remains to be found. In their Howls they spoke for something perennially important: that moment when we take stock of our time and measure it against the deepest yearnings of our inner selves and the most inspired creations of our prophetic ancestors. The Beats respected words. They knew the power of poetry to dream, to give form to a better world. It is that power which still speaks to us, which calls us to craft poems to our own passions, keen elegies to our own agonies, thunder jeremiads against our own jailers. They did it when it was so much harder, when everything was against them; we can when it is all too easy, when the media are a sponge, not a wall.

Because it was so hard, they tried anything to break free: not just drugs but the most destructive ones, like heroin and glue and booze; not just sex but blind-alley affairs with bikers and thieves, gay and straight; not just protest but flag waving for a list of causes left over from throughout the century or yet to be born: ecology, black rights, Eastern thought, meditation, and poetry; not just the search for divine insight but also very limited flirtation on the edge of madness. These extremes exacted a price. There were suicides, and the slow suicide of addiction. There were breakdowns and psychic casualties. The Beats were a moment of inspired agony as well as a program for action. They wrote as visionaries scrying through the madness for a glimpse of God, not as sober social scientists planning out the nation's future.

Beats, like Hippies, also had many imitators, copycats, pretenders. Being a Beat was a way to disdain society, to seek free love, to ennoble utterance as art. There was plenty of posing and posturing in the coffee shops. Many soon tired of the drugs and self-destruction. But the poets represented here, even when their writing came in a rush, full of fragments and momentary thoughts, were not fakes. They challenged America because they knew so much about other places and times, other peoples and cultures, not because it was a lazy way to easy art.

If you want to know more about how the Beat poets actually lived their lives, who inspired them, or why these particular events and people meant so much to them, you can read the biographies and studies listed in the back. If you want to understand the poetry, you need merely to read it, with an open mind and an open ear.

Neal Cassady was famous as a Beat. He searched with Jack Kerouac for the soul of America; he then drove the bus named "Further" that Ken Kesey's group of Merry Pranksters used on their own expedition (recounted in Tom Wolfe's classic book on the Hippies, *The Electric Kool-Aid*

Acid Test). He passed the torch from one movement to another. In this collection David Kherdian passes his own torch on to you, for you to go Further with your own inspired poetry, your own hymn to your new and ancient heartbeat.

—*Marc H. Aronson*

EAST COAST

HOWL
PART I

for Carl Solomon

I saw the best minds of my generation destroyed by madness,
starving hysterical naked,
dragging themselves through the negro streets at dawn looking for an angry fix,
angelheaded hipsters burning for the ancient heavenly con-
nection to the starry dynamo in the machinery of night,
who poverty and tatters and hollow-eyed and high sat up
smoking in the supernatural darkness of cold-water flats
floating across the tops of cities contemplating jazz,
who bared their brains to Heaven under the El and saw
Mohammedan angels staggering on tenement roofs illuminated,
who passed through universities with radiant cool eyes hal-
lucinating Arkansas and Blake-light tragedy among the
scholars of war,
who were expelled from the academies for crazy & publishing
obscene odes on the windows of the skull,
who cowered in unshaven rooms in underwear, burning their
money in wastebaskets and listening to the Terror
through the wall,
who got busted in their pubic beards returning through
Laredo with a belt of marijuana for New York,
who ate fire in paint hotels or drank turpentine in Paradise
Alley, death, or purgatoried their torsos night after night

with dreams, with drugs, with waking nightmares, alcohol
     and cock and endless balls,
incomparable blind streets of shuddering cloud and lightning
     in the mind leaping toward poles of Canada & Paterson,
     illuminating all the motionless world of Time between,
Peyote solidities of halls, backyard green tree cemetery
     dawns, wine drunkenness over the rooftops, storefront
     boroughs of teahead joyride neon blinking traffic light,
     sun and moon and tree vibrations in the roaring winter
     dusks of Brooklyn, ashcan rantings and kind king light
     of mind,
who chained themselves to subways for the endless ride from
     Battery to holy Bronx on benzedrine until the noise of
     wheels and children brought them down shuddering
     mouth-wracked and battered bleak of brain all drained
     of brilliance in the drear light of Zoo,
who sank all night in submarine light of Bickford's floated
     out and sat through the stale beer afternoon in desolate
     Fugazzi's, listening to the crack of doom on the hydrogen
     jukebox,
who talked continuously seventy hours from park to pad to
     bar to Bellevue to museum to the Brookyln Bridge,
a lost battalion of platonic conversationalists jumping down
     the stoops off fire escapes off windowsills off Empire
     State out of the moon,
yacketayakking screaming vomiting whispering facts and
     memories and anecdotes and eyeball kicks and shocks
     of hospitals and jails and wars,
whole intellects disgorged in total recall for seven days and
     nights with brilliant eyes, meat for the Synagogue cast
     on the pavement,
who vanished into nowhere Zen New Jersey leaving a trail

    of ambiguous picture postcards of Atlantic City Hall,
suffering Eastern sweats and Tangerian bone-grindings and
    migraines of China under junk-withdrawal in Newark's
    bleak furnished room,
who wandered around and around at midnight in the railroad
    yard wondering where to go, and went, leaving no bro-
    ken hearts,
who lit cigarettes in boxcars boxcars boxcars racketing
    through snow toward lonesome farms in grandfather
    night,
who studied Plotinus Poe St. John of the Cross telepathy and
    bop kaballa because the cosmos instinctively vibrated at
    their feet in Kansas,
who loned it through the streets of Idaho seeking visionary
    indian angels who were visionary indian angels,
who thought they were only mad when Baltimore gleamed
    in supernatural ecstasy,
who jumped in limousines with the Chinaman of Oklahoma
    on the impulse of winter midnight streetlight smalltown
    rain,
who lounged hungry and lonesome through Houston seeking
    jazz or sex or soup, and followed the brilliant Spaniard
    to converse about America and Eternity, a hopeless task,
    and so took ship to Africa,
who disappeared into the volcanoes of Mexico leaving behind
    nothing but the shadow of dungarees and the lava and
    ash of poetry scattered in fireplace Chicago,
who reappeared on the West Coast investigating the F.B.I.
    in beards and shorts with big pacifist eyes sexy in their
    dark skin passing out incomprehensible leaflets,
who burned cigarette holes in their arms protesting the nar-
    cotic tobacco haze of Capitalism,

who distributed Supercommunist pamphlets in Union Square weeping and undressing while the sirens of Los Alamos wailed them down, and wailed down Wall, and the Staten Island ferry also wailed,

who broke down crying in white gymnasiums naked and trembling before the machinery of other skeletons,

who bit detectives in the neck and shrieked with delight in policecars for committing no crime but their own wild cooking pederasty and intoxication,

who howled on their knees in the subway and were dragged off the roof waving genitals and manuscripts,

who let themselves be fucked in the ass by saintly motorcyclists, and screamed with joy,

who blew and were blown by those human seraphim, the sailors, caresses of Atlantic and Caribbean love,

who balled in the morning in the evenings in rosegardens and the grass of public parks and cemeteries scattering their semen freely to whomever come who may,

who hiccupped endlessly trying to giggle but wound up with a sob behind a partition in a Turkish Bath when the blonde & naked angel came to pierce them with a sword,

who lost their loveboys to the three old shrews of fate the one eyed shrew of the heterosexual dollar the one eyed shrew that winks out of the womb and the one eyed shrew that does nothing but sit on her ass and snip the intellectual golden threads of the craftsman's loom,

who copulated ecstatic and insatiate with a bottle of beer a sweetheart a package of cigarettes a candle and fell off the bed, and continued along the floor and down the hall and ended fainting on the wall with a vision of ultimate cunt and come eluding the last gyzym of consciousness,

who sweetened the snatches of a million girls trembling in

the sunset, and were red eyed in the morning but pre-
pared to sweeten the snatch of the sunrise, flashing buttocks under barns and naked in the lake,
who went out whoring through Colorado in myriad stolen
nightcars, N.C., secret hero of these poems, cocksman
and Adonis of Denver—joy to the memory of his innumerable lays of girls in empty lots & diner backyards,
moviehouses' rickety rows, on mountaintops in caves or
with gaunt waitresses in familiar roadside lonely petti-
coat upliftings & especially secret gas-station solipsisms
of johns, & hometown alleys too,
who faded out in vast sordid movies, were shifted in dreams,
woke on a sudden Manhattan, and picked themselves
up out of basements hungover with heartless Tokay and
horrors of Third Avenue iron dreams & stumbled to
unemployment offices,
who walked all night with their shoes full of blood on the
snowbank docks waiting for a door in the East River to
open to a room full of steamheat and opium,
who created great suicidal dramas on the apartment cliff-
banks of the Hudson under the wartime blue floodlight
of the moon & their heads shall be crowned with laurel
in oblivion,
who ate the lamb stew of the imagination or digested the
crab at the muddy bottom of the rivers of Bowery,
who wept at the romance of the streets with their pushcarts
full of onions and bad music,
who sat in boxes breathing in the darkness under the bridge,
and rose up to build harpsichords in their lofts,
who coughed on the sixth floor of Harlem crowned with flame
under the tubercular sky surrounded by orange crates
of theology,
who scribbled all night rocking and rolling over lofty incan-

tations which in the yellow morning were stanzas of gibberish,

who cooked rotten animals lung heart feet borsht & tortillas dreaming of the pure vegetable kingdom,

who plunged themselves under meat trucks looking for an egg,

who threw their watches off the roof to cast their ballot for Eternity outside of Time, & alarm clocks fell on their heads every day for the next decade,

who cut their wrists three times successively unsuccessfully, gave up and were forced to open antique stores where they thought they were growing old and cried,

who were burned alive in their innocent flannel suits on Madison Avenue amid blasts of leaden verse & the tanked-up clatter of the iron regiments of fashion & the nitroglycerine shrieks of the fairies of advertising & the mustard gas of sinister intelligent editors, or were run down by the drunken taxicabs of Absolute Reality,

who jumped off the Brooklyn Bridge this actually happened and walked away unknown and forgotten into the ghostly daze of Chinatown soup alleyways & firetrucks, not even one free beer,

who sang out of their windows in despair, fell out of the subway window, jumped in the filthy Passaic, leaped on negroes, cried all over the street, danced on broken wineglasses barefoot smashed phonograph records of nostalgic European 1930s German jazz finished the whiskey and threw up groaning into the bloody toilet, moans in their ears and the blast of colossal steam-whistles,

who barreled down the highways of the past journeying to each other's hotrod-Golgotha jail-solitude watch or Birmingham jazz incarnation,

who drove crosscountry seventytwo hours to find out if I had
a vision or you had a vision or he had a vision to find
out Eternity,

who journeyed to Denver, who died in Denver, who came
back to Denver & waited in vain, who watched over
Denver & brooded & loned in Denver and finally went
away to find out the Time, & now Denver is lonesome
for her heroes,

who fell on their knees in hopeless cathedrals praying for
each other's salvation and light and breasts, until the
soul illuminated its hair for a second,

who crashed through their minds in jail waiting for impossible
criminals with golden heads and the charm of reality in
their hearts who sang sweet blues to Alcatraz,

who retired to Mexico to cultivate a habit, or Rocky Mount
to tender Buddha or Tangiers to boys or Southern Pacific
to the black locomotive or Harvard to Narcissus to
Woodlawn to the daisychain or grave,

who demanded sanity trials accusing the radio of hypnotism
& were left with their insanity & their hands & a hung
jury,

who threw potato salad at CCNY lecturers on Dadaism and
subsequently presented themselves on the granite steps
of the madhouse with shaven heads and harlequin
speech of suicide, demanding instantaneous lobotomy,

and who were given instead the concrete void of insulin
Metrazol electricity hydrotherapy psychotherapy occu-
pational therapy pingpong & amnesia,

who in humorless protest overturned only one symbolic pingpong table, resting briefly in catatonia,

returning years later truly bald except for a wig of blood, and
tears and fingers, to the visible madman doom of the
wards of the madtowns of the East,

Pilgrim State's Rockland's and Greystone's foetid halls, bickering with the echoes of the soul, rocking and rolling in the midnight solitude-bench dolmen-realms of love, dream of life a nightmare, bodies turned to stone as heavy as the moon;

with mother finally ******, and the last fantastic book flung out of the tenement window, and the last door closed at 4 AM and the last telephone slammed at the wall in reply and the last furnished room emptied down to the last piece of mental furniture, a yellow paper rose twisted on a wire hanger in the closet, and even that imaginary, nothing but a hopeful little bit of hallucination—

ah, Carl, while you are not safe I am not safe, and now you're really in the total animal soup of time—

and who therefore ran through the icy streets obsessed with a sudden flash of the alchemy of the use of the ellipse the catalog the meter & the vibrating plane,

who dreamt and made incarnate gaps in Time & Space through images juxtaposed, and trapped the archangel of the soul between 2 visual images and joined the elemental verbs and set the noun and dash of consciousness together jumping with sensation of Pater Omnipotens Aeterna Deus

to recreate the syntax and measure of poor human prose and stand before you speechless and intelligent and shaking with shame, rejected yet confessing out the soul to conform to the rhythm of thought in his naked and endless head,

the madman bum and angel beat in Time, unknown, yet putting down here what might be left to say in time come after death,

and rose reincarnate in the ghostly clothes of jazz in the

goldhorn shadow of the band and blew the suffering of
   America's naked mind for love into an eli eli lamma
   lamma sabacthani saxophone cry that shivered the cities
   down to the last radio
with the absolute heart of the poem of life butchered out of
   their own bodies good to eat a thousand years.

San Francisco, 1955–1956

DON'T SHOOT THE WARTHOG

A child came to me
swinging an ocean on a stick.
He told me his sister was dead,
I pulled down his pants
and gave him a kick.
I drove him down the streets
down the night of my generation
I screamed his name, his cursed name,
down the streets of my generation
and children lept in joy to the name
and running came.
Mothers and fathers bent their heads to hear;
I screamed the name.

The child trembled, fell,
and staggered up again,
I screamed his name!
And a fury of mothers and fathers
sank their teeth into his brain.
I called to the angels of my generation
on the rooftops, in the alleyways,
beneath the garbage and the stones,
I screamed the name! and they came
and gnawed the child's bones.
I screamed the name: Beauty
Beauty   Beauty   Beauty

THIS WAS MY MEAL

In the peas I saw upside down letters of MONK
And beside it, in the Eyestares of Wine
I saw Olive & Blackhair
   I decided sunset to dine

I cut through the cowbrain and saw Christmas
& my birthday run hand in hand in the snow
I cut deeper
   and Christmas bled to the edge of the plate

I turned to my father
   and he ate my birthday
I drank my milk and saw trees outrun themselves
   valleys outdo themselves
    and no mountain stood a chance of not walking

Dessert came in the spindly hands of stepmother
I wanted to drop fire-engines from my mouth!
But in ran the moonlight and grabbed the prunes.

HELLO

It is disastrous to be a wounded deer.
I'm the most wounded, wolves stalk,
and I have my failures, too.
My flesh is caught on the Inevitable Hook!
As a child I saw many things I did not want to be.
Am I the person I did not want to be?
That talks-to-himself person?
That neighbors-make-fun-of person?
Am I he who, on museum steps, sleeps on his side?
Do I wear the cloth of a man who has failed?
Am I the looney man?
In the great serenade of things,
     am I the most cancelled passage?

THREE

1

The streetsinger is sick
crouched in the doorway, holding his heart.

One less song in the noisy night.

2

Outside the wall
the aged gardener plants his shears
A new young man
has come to snip the hedge

3

Death weeps because Death is human
spending all day in a movie when a child dies.

I AM 25

With a love a madness for Shelley
Chatterton   Rimbaud
and the needy-yap of my youth
          has gone from ear to ear:
          I HATE OLD POETMEN!
Especially old poetmen who retract
who consult other old poetmen
who speak their youth in whispers,
saying:—I did those then
          but that was then
          that was then—
O I would quiet old men
say to them:—I am your friend
          what you once were, thru me
          you'll be again—
Then at night in the confidence of their homes
rip out their apology-tongues
          and steal their poems.

MARRIAGE

Should I get married? Should I be good?
Astound the girl next door with my velvet suit and faustus
    hood?
Don't take her to movies but to cemeteries
tell all about werewolf bathtubs and forked clarinets
then desire her and kiss her and all the preliminaries
and she going just so far and I understanding why
not getting angry saying You must feel! It's beautiful to feel!
Instead take her in my arms lean against an old crooked
    tombstone
and woo her the entire night the constellations in the sky—

When she introduces me to her parents
back straightened, hair finally combed, strangled by a tie,
should I sit knees together on their 3rd degree sofa
and not ask Where's the bathroom?
How else to feel other than I am,
often thinking Flash Gordon soap—
O how terrible it must be for a young man
seated before a family and the family thinking
We never saw him before! He wants our Mary Lou!
After tea and homemade cookies they ask What do you do
    for a living?

Should I tell them: Would they like me then?
Say All right get married, we're losing a daughter
but we're gaining a son—
And should I then ask Where's the bathroom?

O God, and the wedding! All her family and her friends
and only a handful of mine all scroungy and bearded
just wait to get at the drinks and food—
And the priest! he looking at me as if I masturbated
asking me Do you take this woman for your lawful wedded
      wife?
And I trembling what to say say Pie Glue!
I kiss the bride all those corny men slapping me on the back
She's all yours, boy! Ha-ha-ha!
And in their eyes you could see some obscene honeymoon
      going on—

Then all that absurd rice and clanky cans and shoes
Niagara Falls! Hordes of us! Husbands! Wives! Flowers!
      Chocolates!
All streaming into cozy hotels
All going to do the same thing tonight
The indifferent clerk he knowing what was going to happen
The lobby zombies they knowing what
The whistling elevator man he knowing
The winking bellboy knowing
Everybody knowing! I'd be almost inclined not to do
      anything!
Stay up all night! Stare the hotel clerk in the eye!
Screaming: I deny honeymoon! I deny honeymoon!
running rampant into those almost climactic suites
yelling Radio belly! Cat shovel!
O I'd live in Niagara forever! in a dark cave beneath the Falls
I'd sit there the Mad Honeymooner
devising ways to break marriages, a scourge of bigamy
a saint of divorce—

But I should get married I should be good
How nice it'd be to come home to her
and sit by the fireplace and she in the kitchen
aproned young and lovely wanting my baby
and so happy about me she burns the roast beef
and comes crying to me and I get up from my big papa chair
saying Christmas teeth! Radiant brains! Apple deaf!
God what a husband I'd make! Yes, I should get married!
So much to do! like sneaking into Mr Jones' house late
    at night
and cover his golf clubs with 1920 Norwegian books
Like hanging a picture of Rimbaud on the lawnmower
like pasting Tannu Tuvu postage stamps all over the picket
    fence
like when Mrs Kindhead comes to collect for the Community
    Chest
grab her and tell her There are unfavorable omens in
    the sky!
And when the mayor comes to get my vote tell him
When are you going to stop people killing whales!
And when the milkman comes leave him a note in the bottle
Penguin dust, bring me penguin dust, I want penguin dust—

Yet if I should get married and it's Connecticut and snow
and she gives birth to a child and I am sleepless, worn,
up for nights, head bowed against a quiet window, the past
    behind me,

finding myself in the most common of situations a trembling
    man
knowledged with responsibility not twig-smear nor Roman
    coin soup—

O what would that be like!
Surely I'd give it for a nipple a rubber Tacitus
For a rattle a bag of broken Bach records
Tack Della Francesca all over its crib
Sew the Greek alphabet on its bib
And build for its playpen a roofless Parthenon

No, I doubt I'd be that kind of father
not rural not snow no quiet window
but hot smelly tight New York City
seven flights up, roaches and rats in the walls
a fat Reichian wife screeching over potatoes Get a job!
And five nose running brats in love with Batman
And the neighbors all toothless and dry haired
like those hag masses of the 18th century
all wanting to come in and watch TV
The landlord wants his rent
Grocery store Blue Cross Gas & Electric Knights of
        Columbus
Impossible to lie back and dream Telephone snow, ghost
        parking—
No! I should not get married I should never get married!
But—imagine If I were married to a beautiful sophisticated
        woman
tall and pale wearing an elegant black dress and long black
        gloves
holding a cigarette holder in one hand and a highball in the
        other
and we lived high up in a penthouse with a huge window
from which we could see all of New York and ever farther
        on clearer days
No, can't imagine myself married to that pleasant prison
        dream—

O but what about love? I forget love
not that I am incapable of love
it's just that I see love as odd as wearing shoes—
I never wanted to marry a girl who was like my mother
And Ingrid Bergman was always impossible
And there's maybe a girl now but she's already married
And I don't like men and—
but there's got to be somebody!
Because what if I'm 60 years old and not married,
all alone in a furnished room with pee stains on my underwear
and everybody else is married! All the universe married but
    me!

Ah, yet well I know that were a woman possible as I am
    possible
then marriage would be possible—
Like SHE in her lonely alien gaud waiting her Egyptian lover
so I wait—bereft of 2,000 years and the bath of life.

APRIL FOOL BIRTHDAY POEM FOR GRANDPA

Today is your
birthday and I have tried
writing these things before,
but now
in the gathering madness, I want to
thank you
for telling me what to expect
for pulling
no punches, back there in that scrubbed Bronx parlor
thank you
for honestly weeping in time to
innumerable heartbreaking
italian operas for
pulling my hair when I
pulled the leaves off the trees so I'd
know how it feels, we are
involved in it now, revolution, up to our
knees and the tide is rising, I embrace
strangers on the street, filled with their love and
mine, the love you told us had to come or we
die, told them all in that Bronx park, me listening in
spring Bronx dusk, breathing stars, so glorious
to me your white hair, your height your fierce
blue eyes, rare among italians, I stood
a ways off, looking up at you, my grandpa
people listened to, I stand
a ways off listening as I pour out soup

young men with light in their faces
at my table, talking love, talking revolution
which is love, spelled backwards, how
you would love us all, would thunder your anarchist wisdom
at us, would thunder Dante, and Giordano Bruno,
    orderly men
bent to your ends, well I want you to know
we do it for you, and your ilk, for Carlo Tresca,
for Sacco and Vanzetti, without knowing
it, or thinking about it, as we do it for Aubrey Beardsley
Oscar Wilde (all street lights
shall be purple), do it
for Trotsky and Shelley and big/dumb
Kropotkin
Eisenstein's Strike people, Jean Cocteau's ennui,
    we do it for
the stars over the Bronx
that they may look on earth
and not be ashamed.

SONG FOR BABY-O, UNBORN

Sweetheart
when you break thru
you'll find
a poet here
not quite what one would choose.

I won't promise
you'll never go hungry
or that you won't be sad
on this gutted
breaking
globe

but I can show you
baby
enough to love
to break your heart
forever

PULL MY DAISY

Pull my daisy
Tip my cup
Cut my thoughts
for coconuts

Jack my Arden
Gate my shades
Silk my garden
Rose my days

Bone my shadow
Dove my dream
Milk my mind &
Make me cream

Hop my heart on
Harp my height
Hip my angel
Hype my light

Heal the raindrop
Sow the eye
Woe the worm
Work the wise

Stop the hoax
Where's the wake
What's the box
How's the Hicks

Rob my locker
Lick my rocks
Rack my lacks
Lark my looks

Whore my door
Beat my beer
Craze my hair
Bare my poor

Say my oops
Ope my shell
Roll my bones
Ring my bell

Pope my parts
Pop my pet
Poke my pap
Pit my plum

1951, 1958? 1961

HYMN

And when you showed me Brooklyn Bridge
  in the morning,
    Ah God,

And the people slipping on ice in the street,
twice,
    twice,
        two different people
        came over, goin to work,
        so earnest and tryful,
        clutching their pitiful
        morning Daily News
        slip on the ice & fall
        both inside 5 minutes
        and I cried I cried

That's when you taught me tears, Ah
  God in the morning,
    Ah Thee

And me leaning on the lamppost wiping
eyes,
    eyes,
        nobody's know I'd cried
        or woulda cared anyway
        but O I saw my father
        and my grandfather's mother
        and the long lines of chairs
        and tear-sitters and dead,
        Ah me, I knew God You
        had better plans than that

So whatever plan you have for me
Splitter of majesty
Make it short
  brief
Make it snappy
  bring me home to the Eternal Mother
  today

At your service anyway,
  (and until)

I GOT A PHONE CALL

I got a phone call,
                    from my heart
its tune I knew before it rang
no dime here, or operators to interfear
could an opera singer be down there
or my love thats very small
                              but pure in there.
it had a crying ring
I wanted to answer
                  but couldent but can & did
yet delayed for fear has a ring around everyones brow, or
      under each eye
the ring rang on
I poundered why?
could I want me?
could peter call peter from such a small place?
hardly room for a hope diamond
or a pillow race
would splashy ink pudle my face as I picked up the phone
the humming time stopped
the noise came clear
I waited in fear

1959 NYC

CREEDMOOR STATE MENTAL HOSPITAL
NIGHT SHIFT LOOK & MOP

By now hes dead & burried
    in the corner of my eye—
He was an old italian in the mad house
ward—every day I would see him—
Half blind & a palsy hand
    dressed in grey state robe—
Almost morning I meet him
he would say come, Peter—take me to the subway—
    give me a
nickle—we go to my old
    Barber shop—come, lets go now
One day I said ok & led him down the hall
    letting him believe I was takeing him to Brooklyn
    but when we reached the door—
    I was only an attendant
    not a doctor—
Hes a dead man now & burried
in the corner of my eye
& he taught me two italian words
Pichada & mangia
Piss & food

1959 NYC

WHY TRY?

And she was brown
And she always dressed and wore brown
And she had a fine brown body
And she had two beautiful brown eyes
And she would sit in the Beat Cafe
on her brown behind on a hard brown bench
and listen to brown sounds entertain her brown thoughts
And she would often double cross her big brown legs
And reveal her beautiful brown pleasing knees
And as she sat in the Beat Cafe on her brown behind on the
    hard brown bench
And listening to brown sounds coming from
    brown entertainers of brown bohemia
I   saw   a young white girl   throw away her
        brand new jar of

                            suntan lotion   and sigh:

                                    WHY TRY?

FOR HETTIE

My wife is left-handed.
Which implies a fierce de-
termination. A complete other
worldliness. IT'S WEIRD BABY
The way some folks
are always trying to be different.
A sin & a shame.

But then, she's been a bohemian
all her life . . . black stockings,
refusing to take orders. I sit
patiently, trying to tell her
what's right. TAKE THAT DAMM
PENCIL OUTTA THAT HAND. YOU'RE
RITING BACKWARDS. & such. But
to no avail. & it shows
in her work. Left-handed coffee,
left-handed eggs: when she comes
in at night . . . it's her left hand
offered for me to kiss. DAMM.

& now her belly droops over the seat.
They say it's a child. But
I ain't quite so sure.

GREENWICH VILLAGE OF MY DREAMS

A rose in a stone.
Chariots on the West Side Highway.
Blues in the Soviet Union.
Onions in times square.
A Japanese in Chinatown.
A soup sandwich.
A Hudson terraplane.
Chess in a Catskill bungalow.
Awnings in Atlanta.
Lewisohn stadium in the blackout.
Brooklyn beneath the East River.
        the waves passover.
The Battery in startling sunlight.
Kleins in Ohrbachs.
Love on the dole, Roosevelt not elected.
Hoover under the 3rd Ave El
Joe Gould kissing Maxwell Bodenheim
        & puffing on his pipe
Edna Millay feeling Edmund Wilson
Charlie Parker & Ted Joans talking
        in Sheridan Sq Park & its cold man!
The Cedar St Bar with Cedars in it
        & authors crashing against the cedars
The Chase Manhattan Bank closed
        down for repairs. To open as the
        new Waldorf Cafeteria.
Lionel Trilling kissing Allen Ginsberg
        after great Reading in the Gaslight

The Limelight changes its name to
    the Electric Light & features
    Charlie Chaplin as a s(w)inging
    waiter
Edgar Allan Poe becoming the dentist
    in the Waverly dispensary & giving
    everyone free nitrous oxide high
Louis getting thrown out of Louis'
San Remo stepping up to the bar &
    asking for a wet Martini
The Charleston on Charles St
    featuring my Sister Eileen
    & the Kronstadt sailors.
Max Eastman & John Reed
    buying Gungawala hashish candy
    at the German Delicatessen on 6th
    Ave & West 4th Street.
Tourists bringing pictures to sell
    to artists in their annual disposition.
Civilians telling cops to move on
Coffeehouses that sell brandy
    in their coffee cups
Eugene O'Neill insisting on coffee
John Barrymore in offbroadway Hamlet
Walt Whitman cruising on MacDougal
Ike & Mamie drunk in Minettas
Khrushchev singing peat bog soldiers
    in the circle (with a balalaika)
Everybody kissing & hugging squeezing
Khrushchev & Eisenhower a big fat kiss
The world an art
Life a joy
The village come to life again

I wake up singing
I that dwell in New York
Sweet song bless my mouth
Beauty bless my eyes

*Song of the world
Fly forth from dreams!*

How beautiful is love
And the fruit thereof
Holy holy holy
A kiss and a star

THREE PRAYERS

1.

o do not let our children
as you let us, grow
without the help of hatred

do not let the violence of their souls
destroy their souls
let them sing it out

against us?
            what else?

2.

grant that the walls may fall
catching within their ruin
all the ones who've lived in sanctuary
& from their vantage point have
grabbed us
pumped into
our blood
a hideous drug of their own invention
                              & forced us to be

to accept us
while we despised
them &
ourselves
          grant that the walls may get them
as they now have us

3.

a personal prayer / let me have the strength
to make the scene
& still not harshly warp
my true sound

let me gain power over that power
that tries to kill me

loosen the root of death within my head
& let me get my hands on it, & pull, & pull

the curvature of the thing

her lower lip
was like an orange
mint. and
i was a crying
little boy
in the candy store.

THE CUTTING PROW

For Henri Matisse

The genius was 81
Fearful of blindness
Caught in a wheelchair
Staring at death

But the Angel of Mercy
gave him a year
to scissor some shapes
to soothe the scythe

and shriek!   shriek!

　　　became

　　　swawk!   swawk!
　　　　the peace of
　　　　　　scissors.

There was something besides
the inexpressible

　　　thrill

of cutting a beautiful shape—

for
Each thing had a "sign"
Each thing had a "symbol"
Each thing had a cutting form

—swawk swawkk—

to scissor seize.

"One must study an object a long time,"
  the genius said,
"to know what its sign is."

The scissors were his scepter
The cutting
was as the prow of a barque
to sail him away.

There's a photograph
        which shows him
sitting in his wheelchair
bare foot touching the floor
drawing with crisscross steel
a shape in the gouache

His helper sits near him
till he hands her the form
to pin to the wall

He points with a stick
how he wants it adjusted
This way and that,
        minutitudinous

The last blue iris blooms at
the top of its stalk

      scissors/sceptor
       cutting/prow

(*sung*)

Ah, keep those scissors flashing in the
World of Forms, Henri Matisse

The cutting of the scissors
was the prow of a boat
      to take him away
The last blue iris
    blooms at the top
       on a warm spring day

Ah, keep those scissors flashing in the
World of Forms, Henri Matisse

Sitting in a wheelchair
bare feet touching the floor
Angel of Mercy
      pushed him over
       next to Plato's Door

    Scissor scepter cutting prow
    Scissor scepter cutting prow
    Scissor scepter cutting prow
    Scissor scepter cutting prow

✂
ahh
swawk swawk

✂
ahh
swawk swawk

✂
ahh
swawk swawk

OUR PAST

You said my life was meant to run from yours as streams
from the river.
You are the ocean I won't run to you
We were standing on Arapahoe in front of the Silver Saddle
Motel
They had no rooms for us
I wore the high red huaraches of Mexico & a long skirt of
patches
You had traveled back from Utah
I thought of the Salt Lakes, seeing them once from a plane
they were like blank patches in the mind or bandaged
places of the heart
I felt chilly
I had just ridden down the mountain with a car full of poets,
one terrified of the shifting heights, the dark, the moun-
tains, he said, closing in
I said Wait for me, but I have to go here first, or, it's too
complicated, some kind of stalling because I wanted you
You were direct, you were traveling light, your feet were
light, your hair was light, you were attentive
Were you rushing me?
We walked by the stream, you held me, I said I have to get
back soon because he's waiting, maybe he's suffering
I think the moon was waning
You walked me back along 9th Street under dark trees
The night we'd met, June 6, we'd come out of the New York
Church to observe a performer jumping over signposts

I was with my friend, a mentor, much older
You were introduced to him, to me
You said you'd followed me out from that night to where the
continent divides, where my heart divided
I wrote poems to you in Santa Fe
You followed me all the way to Kitkitdizze
I waited for you, when you came I was away
I drove miles to speak with you on the telephone
I met you in Nevada City after nearly turning back to put
out a fire
We went to Alta, the lake of your childhood
I wanted to stay forever in the big room with all the little
white beds, like a nursery
You were like first love
All the impossibilities were upon us
We never had enough time
In Palo Alto where they name the streets after poets I ad-
mired your mother's pretty oriental things
In San Francisco we ate hurriedly at the joint near the opera
house
I lied about going to Chicago for your birthday in New York
I lied about spending Christmas with you in Cherry Valley
I will never forget the dance you did to the pipes of Finbar
Furey on New Year's day. You kept your torso bent to
protect your heart
Then I moved to Colorado
We met and sat in the yard of a friend's brother's house in
Missoula, Montana
It's wonderful the way this city turns serenely into country
with no fuss, the city is shed, or is it the other way
around, the country falls off into the city?

It was how I wanted us to shed our other lives at least when
we were together
In that yard you made me feel our situation was intolerable
We seemed to be in constant pain
When we parted at the small airport early that morning my
heart finally ripped
In the spring back in New York, things got darker
I was sick, my head was swollen
I remember reading to you about the Abidharma on a
mattress
I had trouble speaking
I behaved badly and embarrassed you at the uptown party
A part of you had left me for good
You'd given your loft over to weekly parties
You were having a public life. I felt you were turning into
me
I wanted our private romance
Was I being straight with you, I wondered?
I let you think things of me that weren't true. You thought
I was wise & couldn't be hurt
Then I had the person I lived with and what could be
said about that?
That summer you visited my hotel in Boulder. We slept on
separate mattresses. I felt I was trying to imprison you
and after you left I couldn't go back there for days. When
I did I found a dead bird had gotten entrapped, struggled
fiercely to get out
The following winter I waited for you in sub zero cold, wearing black. I was told you'd come & gone. You didn't
return. We spoke on the phone a long time.
I said I was going home and falling in love with someone
else. You said It sounds like you want to

My mother heard me crying and came to me in the bathtub
and said O don't, it breaks my heart! I told her I was
going to the hell for a while I'd often made for others,
karma works that way. Bosh karma she said
We've met briefly in Portland, Oregon and New York
We've corresponded all this time, following the details of
each other's lives and work
Your father has recently died
My baby son grows stronger
The last time I saw you you were standing on my street corner
As I came toward you you said What a youthful gait you have

ON THE
ROAD

from *ON THE ROAD*

The parties were enormous; there were at least a hundred people at a basement apartment in the West Nineties. People overflowed into the cellar compartments near the furnace. Something was going on in every corner, on every bed and couch—not an orgy but just a New Year's party with frantic screaming and wild radio music. There was even a Chinese girl. Dean ran like Groucho Marx from group to group, digging everybody. Periodically we rushed out to the car to pick up more people. Damion came. Damion is the hero of my New York gang, as Dean is the chief hero of the Western. They immediately took a dislike to each other. Damion's girl suddenly socked Damion on the jaw with a roundhouse right. He stood reeling. She carried him home. Some of our mad newspaper friends came in from the office with bottles. There was a tremendous and wonderful snowstorm going on outside. Ed Dunkel met Lucille's sister and disappeared with her; I forgot to say that Ed Dunkel is a very smooth man with the women. He's six foot four, mild, affable, agreeable, bland, and delightful. He helps women on with their coats. That's the way to do things. At five o'clock in the morning we were all rushing through the backyard of a tenement and climbing in through a window of an apartment where a huge party was going on. At dawn we were back at Tom Saybrook's. People were drawing pictures and drinking stale beer. I slept on a couch with a girl called Mona in my arms. Great groups filed in from the old Columbia Campus bar. Everything in life, all the faces of life, were piling into the same dank room.

At Ian MacArthur's the party went on. Ian MacArthur is a wonderful sweet fellow who wears glasses and peers out of them with delight. He began to learn "Yes!" to everything, just like Dean at this time, and hasn't stopped since. To the wild sounds of Dexter Gordon and Wardell Gray blowing "The Hunt," Dean and I played catch with Marylou over the couch; she was no small doll either. Dean went around with no undershirt, just his pants, barefoot, till it was time to hit the car and fetch more people. Everything happened. We found the wild, ecstatic Rollo Greb and spent a night at his house on Long Island. Rollo lives in a nice house with his aunt; when she dies the house is all his. Meanwhile she refuses to comply with any of his wishes and hates his friends. He brought this ragged gang of Dean, Marylou, Ed, and me, and began a roaring party. The woman prowled upstairs; she threatened to call the police. "Oh, shut up, you old bag!" yelled Greb. I wondered how he could live with her like this. He had more books than I've ever seen in all my life—two libraries, two rooms loaded from floor to ceiling around all four walls, and such books as the Apocryphal Something-or-Other in ten volumes. He played Verdi operas and panto-mimed them in his pajamas with a great rip down the back. He didn't give a damn about anything. He is a great scholar who goes reeling down the New York waterfront with original seventeenth-century musical manuscripts under his arm, shouting. He crawls like a big spider through the streets. His excitement blew out of his eyes in stabs of fiendish light. He rolled his neck in spastic ecstasy. He lisped, he writhed, he flopped, he moaned, he howled, he fell back in despair. He could hardly get a word out, he was so excited with life. Dean stood before him with head bowed, repeating over and over again. "Yes . . . Yes . . . Yes." He took me into a corner. "That

Rollo Greb is the greatest, most wonderful of all. That's what I was trying to tell you—that's what I want to be. I want to be like him. He's never hung-up, he goes every direction, he lets it all out, he knows time, he has nothing to do but rock back and forth. Man, he's the end! You see, if you go like him all the time you'll finally get it."

"Get what?"

"IT! IT! I'll tell you—now no time, we have no time now." Dean rushed back to watch Rollo Greb some more.

George Shearing, the great jazz pianist, Dean said, was exactly like Rollo Greb. Dean and I went to see Shearing at Birdland in the midst of the long, mad weekend. The place was deserted, we were the first customers, ten o'clock. Shearing came out, blind, led by the hand to his keyboard. He was a distinguished-looking Englishman with a stiff white collar, slightly beefy, blond, with a delicate English-summer's-night air about him that came out in the first rippling sweet number he played as the bass-player leaned to him reverently and thrummed the beat. The drummer, Denzil Best, sat motionless except for his wrists snapping the brushes. And Shearing began to rock; a smile broke over his ecstatic face; he began to rock in the piano seat, back and forth, slowly at first, then the beat went up, and he began rocking fast, his left foot jumped up with every beat, his neck began to rock crookedly, he brought his face down to the keys, he pushed his hair back, his combed hair dissolved, he began to sweat. The music picked up. The bass-player hunched over and socked it in, faster and faster, it seemed faster and faster, that's all. Shearing began to play his chords; they rolled out of the piano in great rich showers, you'd think the man wouldn't have time to line them up. They rolled and rolled like the sea. Folks yelled for him to "Go!" Dean was sweating; the sweat poured down his collar. "There he is! That's him! Old God! Old God Shearing! Yes! Yes! Yes!" And Shearing was conscious of the madman behind him, he could hear every one of Dean's gasps and imprecations, he could sense it though he couldn't see. "That's right!" Dean said. "Yes!" Shearing smiled; he rocked. Shearing rose from the piano, dripping with sweat; these were his great 1949 days before he became cool and commercial. When he was gone Dean pointed to the empty piano seat. "God's empty chair," he said. On the piano a horn sat; its golden shadow made a strange reflection along the desert caravan painted on the wall behind the drums. God was gone; it was the silence of his departure. It was a rainy night. It was the myth of the rainy night. Dean was popeyed with awe. This madness would lead nowhere. I didn't know what was happening to me, and I suddenly realized it was only the tea that we were smoking; Dean had bought some in New York. It made me think that everything was about to arrive—the moment when you know all and everything is decided forever.

I had to wake him up; I couldn't get the car started to dump it somewhere far off. He stumbled out of bed, wearing just his jockey shorts, and we got in the car together, while the kids giggled from the windows, and went bouncing and flying straight over the hard alfalfa-rows at the end of the road whomp-ti-whomp till finally the car couldn't take any more and stopped dead under an old cottonwood near the old mill. "Can't go any farther," said Dean simply and got out and started walking back over the cornfield, about half a mile, in his shorts in the moonlight. We got back to the house and he went to sleep. Everything was in a horrible mess, all of Denver, my woman friend, cars, children, poor

Frankie, the living room splattered with beer and cans, and I tried to sleep. A cricket kept me awake for some time. At night in this part of the West the stars, as I had seen them in Wyoming, are big as roman candles and as lonely as the Prince of the Dharma who's lost his ancestral grove and journeys across the spaces between points in the handle of the Big Dipper, trying to find it again. So they slowly wheeled the night, and then long before actual sunrise the great red light appeared far over the dun bleak land toward West Kansas and the birds took up their trill above Denver.

"Now this is the first time we've been along and in a position to talk for years," said Dean. And he talked all night. As in a dream, we were zooming back through sleeping Washington and back in the Virginia wilds, crossing the Appomattox River at daybreak, pulling up at my brother's door at eight A.M. And all this time Dean was tremendously excited about everything he saw, everything he talked about, every detail of every moment that passed. He was out of his mind with real belief. "And of course now no one can tell us that there is no God. We've passed through all forms. You remember, Sal, when I first came to New York and I wanted Chad King to teach me about Nietzsche. You see how long ago? Everything is fine, God exists, we know time. Everything since the Greeks has been predicated wrong. You can't make it with geometry and geometrical systems of thinking. It's all *this!*" He wrapped his finger in his fist; the car hugged the line straight and true. "And not only that but we both understand that I couldn't have time to explain why I know and you know God exists." At one point I moaned about life's troubles—how poor my family was, how much I wanted to help Lucille, who was also poor and had a daughter. "Troubles, you see, is the generalization-word for what God exists in. The thing is not to get hung-up. My head rings!" he cried, clasping his head. He rushed out of the car like Groucho Marx to get cigarettes—that furious, ground-hugging walk with the coattails flying, except that he had no coattails. "Since Denver, Sal, a lot of things—Oh, the things—I've thought and thought. I used to be in reform school all the time, I was a young punk, asserting myself—stealing cars a psychological expression of my position, hincty to show. All my jail-problems are pretty straight now. As far as I know I shall never be in jail again. The rest is not my fault." We passed a little kid who was throwing stones at the cars in the road. "Think of it," said Dean. "One day he'll put a stone through a man's windshield and the man will crash and die—all on account of that little kid. You see what I mean? God exists without qualms. As we roll along this way I am positive beyond doubt that everything will be taken care of for us—that even you, as you drive, fearful of the wheel" (I hated to drive and drove carefully)—"the thing will go along of itself and you won't go off the road and I can sleep. Furthermore we know America, we're at home; I can go anywhere in America and get what I want because it's the same in every corner, I know the people, I know what they do. We give and take and go in the incredibly complicated sweetness zigzagging every side." There was nothing clear about the things he said, but what he meant to say was somehow made pure and clear. He used the word "pure" a great deal. I had never dreamed Dean would become a mystic. These were the first days of his mysticism, which would lead to the strange, ragged W. C. Fields saintliness of his later days.

In Oakland I had a beer among the bums of a saloon with a wagon wheel in front of it, and I was on the road again. I walked clear across Oakland to get on the Fresno road. Two rides took me to Bakersfield, four hundred miles south. The first was the mad one, with a burly blond kid in a souped-up rod. "See that toe?" he said as he gunned the heap to eighty and passed everybody on the road. "Look at it." It was swathed in bandages. "I just had it amputated this morning. The bastards wanted me to stay in the hospital. I packed my bag and left. What's a toe?" Yes, indeed, I said to myself, look out now, and I hung on. You never saw a driving fool like that. He made Tracy in no time. Tracy is a railroad town; brakemen eat surly meals in diners by the tracks. Trains howl away across the valley. The sun goes down long and red. All the magic names of the valley unrolled—Manteca, Madera, all the rest. Soon it got dusk, a grapy dusk, a purple dusk over tangerine groves and long melon fields; the sun the color of pressed grapes, slashed and burgundy red, the fields the color of love and Spanish mysteries. I stuck my head out the window and took deep breaths of the fragrant air. It was the most beautiful of all moments. The madman was a brakeman with the Southern Pacific and he lived in Fresno; his father was also a brakeman. He lost his toe in the Oakland yards, switching, I didn't quite understand how. He drove me into buzzing Fresno and let me off by the south side of town. I went for a quick Coke in a little grocery by the tracks, and here came a melancholy Armenian youth along the red boxcars, and just at that moment a locomotive howled, and I said to myself, Yes, yes, Saroyan's town.

I had to go south; I got on the road. A man in a brand-new pickup truck picked me up. He was from Lubbock, Texas, and was in the trailer business. "You want to buy a trailer?" he asked me. "Any time, look me up." He told stories about his father in Lubbock. "One night my old man left the day's receipts settin on top of the safe, plumb forgot. What happened—a thief came in the night, acetylene torch and all, broke open the safe, riffled up the papers, kicked over a few chairs, and left. And that thousand dollars was settin right there on top of the safe, what do you know about that?"

He let me off south of Bakersfield, and then my adventure began. It grew cold. I put on the flimsy Army raincoat I'd bought in Oakland for three dollars and shuddered in the road. I was standing in front of an ornate Spanish-style motel that was lit like a jewel. The cars rushed by, LA-bound. I gestured frantically. It was too cold. I stood there till midnight, two hours straight, and cursed and cursed. It was just like Stuart, Iowa, again. There was nothing to do but spend a little over two dollars for a bus the remaining miles to Los Angeles. I walked back along the highway to Bakersfield and into the station, and sat down on a bench.

I had bought my ticket and was waiting for the LA bus when all of a sudden I saw the cutest little Mexican girl in slacks come cutting across my sight. She was in one of the buses that had just pulled in with a big sigh of airbrakes; it was discharging passengers for a rest stop. Her breasts stuck out straight and true; her little flanks looked delicious; her hair was long and lustrous black; and her eyes were great big blue things with timidities inside. I wished I was on her bus. A pain stabbed my heart, as it did every time I saw a girl I loved who was going the opposite direction in this too-big world. The announcer called the LA bus. I picked up my bag and got on, and who should be sitting there alone but the Mexican girl. I dropped right opposite her and began scheming right off. I was so lonely, so sad, so tired, so quivering, so broken, so beat, that I got up my courage, the courage necessary to approach a strange girl, and acted. Even then I spent five minutes beating my thighs in the dark as the bus rolled down the road.

You gotta, you gotta or you'll die! Damn fool, talk to her! What's wrong with you? Aren't you tired enough of yourself by now? And before I knew what I was doing I leaned across the aisle to her (she was trying to sleep on the seat) and said, "Miss, would you like to use my raincoat for a pillow?"

She looked up with a smile and said, "No, thank you very much."

I sat back, trembling; I lit a butt. I waited till she looked at me, with a sad little sidelook of love, and I got right up and leaned over her. "May I sit with you, miss?"

"If you wish."

And this I did. "Where going?"

"LA." I loved the way she said "LA"; I love the way every-body says "LA" on the Coast; it's their one and only golden town when all is said and done.

"That's where I'm going too!" I cried. "I'm very glad you let me sit with you, I was very lonely and I've been traveling a hell of a lot." And we settled down to telling our stories. Her story was this: She had a husband and child. The husband beat her, so she left him, back at Sabinal, south of Fresno, and was going to LA to live with her sister awhile. She left her little son with her family, who were grape-pickers and lived in a shack in the vineyards. She had nothing to do but brood and get mad. I felt like putting my arms around her right away. We talked and talked. She said she loved to talk with me. Pretty soon she was saying she wished she could go to New York too. "Maybe we could!" I laughed. The bus groaned up Grapevine Pass and then we were coming down into the great sprawls of light. Without coming to any par-ticular agreement we began holding hands, and in the same way it was mutely and beautifully and purely decided that when I got my hotel room in LA she would be beside me. I ached all over for her; I leaned my head in her beautiful hair. Her little shoulders drove me mad; I hugged her and hugged her. And she loved it.

"I love love," she said, closing her eyes. I promised her beautiful love. I gloated over her. Our stories were told; we subsided into silence and swept anticipatory thoughts. It was as simple as that. You could have all your Peaches and Bettys and Marylous and Ritas and Camilles and Inezes in this world; this was my girl and my kind of girlsoul, and I told her that.

So in America when the sun goes down and I sit on the old broken-down river pier watching the long, long skies over New Jersey and sense all that raw land that rolls in one unbelievable huge bulge over to the West Coast, and all that road going, all the people dreaming in the immensity of it, and in Iowa I know by now the children must be crying in the land where they let the children cry, and tonight the stars'll be out, and don't you know that God is Pooh Bear? the evening star must be drooping and shedding her sparkler dims on the prairie, which is just before the coming of complete night that blesses the earth, darkens all rivers, cups the peaks and folds the final shore in, and nobody, nobody knows what's going to happen to anybody besides the forlorn rags of growing old, I think of Dean Moriarty, I even think of Old Dean Moriarty the father we never found, I think of Dean Moriarty.

FAMILIES IN IOWA

Dad's crewcut wig smelled of candies.
Son said hug me here, hi pal, voom gee good.
Then Niece fell from the glassed-in crisper
"beset by the junebug plague"—namely Uncle.
Down at the incinerator Nephew exposed himself
But Auntie was licking whips in the silo,
Whips named Sis. The Twins finished their baby-shaped
Popsicle and Cousin and Brother rubbed and rubbed
Against Granny's earache. How mossy, she wept.

Bye now, Mother announced. And so everyone left for
     institutions,
Stadiums, subways, mountains and many such zany palaces.
Mother unzipped and out leapt Mom Mummy and Mammy
And together those four drove
To the experimental cemetery
To have fun.

CHICAGO POEM

I lived here nearly 5 years before I could
    meet the middle western day with anything approaching
Dignity. It's a place that lets you
    understand why the Bible is the way it is:
Proud people cannot live here.

The land's too flat. Ugly sullen and big it
    pounds men down past humbleness. They
Stoop at 35 possibly cringing from the heavy and
    terrible sky. In country like this there
Can be no God but Jahweh.

In the mills and refineries of its south side Chicago
    passes its natural gas in flames
Bouncing like bunsens from stacks a hundred feet high.
    The stench stabs at your eyeballs.
The whole sky green and yellow backdrop for the skeleton
    steel of a bombed-out town.

Remember the movies in grammar school? The goggled men
    doing strong things in
Showers of steel-spark? The dark screen cracking light
    and the furnace door opening with a
Blast of orange like a sunset? Or an orange?

It was photographed by a fairy, thrilled as a girl, or
    a Nazi who wished there were people
Behind that door (hence the remote beauty), but Sievers,
    whose old man spent most of his life in there,
Remembers a "nigger in a red T-shirt pissing into the
    black sand."

It was 5 years until I could afford to recognize the ferocity.
    Friends helped me. Then I put some
Love into my house. Finally I found some quiet lakes
    and a farm where they let me shoot pheasant.

Standing in the boat one night I watched the lake go
    absolutely flat. Smaller than raindrops, and only
Here and there, the feeding rings of fish were visible a
    hundred yards away—and the Blue Gill caught that
    afternoon
Lifted from its northern lake like a tropical! Jewel at its ear
    Belly gold so bright you'd swear he had a
Light in there. His color faded with his life. A small
    green fish . . .

All things considered, it's a gentle and undemanding
    planet, even here. Far gentler
Here than any of a dozen other places. The trouble is
    always and only with what we build on top of it.

There's nobody else to blame. You can't fix it and you
    can't make it go away. It does no good appealing
To some ill-invented Thunderer
    Brooding above some unimaginable crag . . .

It's ours. Right down to the last small hinge it
        all depends for its existence
Only and utterly upon our sufferance.

Driving back I saw Chicago rising in its gases and I
        knew again that never will the
Man be made to stand against this pitiless, unparallel
        monstrocity. It
Snuffles on the beach of its Great Lake like a
        blind, red, rhinoceros.
It's already running us down.

You can't fix it. You can't make it go away.
        I don't know what you're going to do about it,
But I know what I'm going to do about it. I'm just
        going to walk away from it. Maybe
A small part of it will die if I'm not around

        feeding it anymore.

POETS HITCHHIKING ON THE HIGHWAY

Of course I tried to tell him
but he cranked his head
    without an excuse.
I told him the sky chases
    the sun
And he smiled and said:
    "What's the use."
I was feeling like a demon
    again
So I said: "But the ocean chases
    the fish."
This time he laughed
    and said: "Suppose the
        strawberry were
            pushed into a mountain."
After that I knew the
    war was on—
So we fought:
He said: "The apple-cart like a
             broomstick-angel
      snaps & splinters
          old dutch shoes."
I said: "Lightning will strike the old oak
    and free the fumes!"
He said: "Mad street with no name."
I said: "Bald killer! Bald killer! Bald killer!"

He said, getting real mad,
     "Firestoves! Gas! Couch!"
I said, only smiling,
     "I know God would turn back his head
     if I sat quietly and thought."
We ended by melting away,
  hating the air!

UNTITLED

Where is the child, who
one play-ripe summer evening,
forgot to say his prayers;
thus plunging his small soul
into stark disfavor
of a demanding God-head;
not to say the more imminent,
but less terrifying, rage
of a frigid, Christian mother?

He curls in a twilight corner,
dusty knees tucked under him,
absorbed in self-reprisal;
barely hearing the faint tinkle
of ice-cubes in martinis,
or the muted telling-whispers
above the shrill cacophony
of tumbling grass-stained children,
who don't forget that God is Love.

POEM IN PRAISE OF MY HUSBAND (TAOS)

I suppose it hasn't been easy living with me either,
with my piques, and ups and downs, my need for privacy
leo pride and weeping in bed when you're trying to sleep
and you, interrupting me in the middle of a thousand poems
did I call the insurance people? the time you stopped a poem
in the middle of our drive over the nebraska hills and
into colorado, odetta singing, the whole world singing in me
the triumph of our revolution in the air
me about to get that down, and you
you saying something about the carburetor
so that it all went away

but we cling to each other
as if each thought the other was the raft
and he adrift alone, as in this mud house
not big enough, the walls dusting down around us, a fine
    dust rain
counteracting the good, high air, and stuffing our nostrils
we hang our pictures of the several worlds:
new york collage, and san francisco posters,
set out our japanese dishes, chinese knives
hammer small indian marriage cloths into the adobe
we stumble thru silence into each other's gut

blundering thru from one wrong place to the next
like kids who snuck out to play on a boat at night
and the boat slipped from its moorings, and they look at the
    stars
about which they know nothing, to find out
where they are going

WEST
COAST

AMERICA

America I've given you all and now I'm nothing.
America two dollars and twentyseven cents January 17, 1956.
I can't stand my own mind.
America when will we end the human war?
Go fuck yourself with your atom bomb.
I don't feel good don't bother me.
I won't write my poem till I'm in my right mind.
America when will you be angelic?
When will you take off your clothes?
When will you look at yourself through the grave?
When will you be worthy of your million Trotskyites?
America why are your libraries full of tears?
America when will you send your eggs to India?
I'm sick of your insane demands.
When can I go into the supermarket and buy what I need
    with my good looks?
America after all it is you and I who are perfect not the next
    world.
Your machinery is too much for me.
You made me want to be a saint.
There must be some other way to settle this argument.
Burroughs is in Tangiers I don't think he'll come back it's
    sinister.
Are you being sinister or is this some form of practical joke?
I'm trying to come to the point.
I refuse to give up my obsession.
America stop pushing I know what I'm doing.

America the plum blossoms are falling.

I haven't read the newspapers for months, everyday somebody goes on trial for murder.

America I feel sentimental about the Wobblies.

America I used to be a communist when I was a kid I'm not sorry.

I smoke marijuana every chance I get.

I sit in my house for days on end and stare at the roses in the closet.

When I go to Chinatown I get drunk and never get laid.

My mind is made up there's going to be trouble.

You should have seen me read Marx.

My psychoanalyst thinks I'm perfectly right.

I won't say the Lord's Prayer.

I have mystical visions and cosmic vibrations.

America I still haven't told you what you did to Uncle Max after he came over from Russia.

I'm addressing you.

Are you going to let your emotional life be run by Time Magazine?

I'm obsessed by Time Magazine.

I read it every week.

Its cover stares at me every time I slink past the corner candystore.

I read it in the basement of the Berkeley Public Library.

It's always telling me about responsibility. Businessmen are serious. Movie producers are serious. Everybody's serious but me.

It occurs to me that I am America.

I am talking to myself again.

Asia is rising against me.

I haven't got a chinaman's chance.

I'd better consider my national resources.

My national resources consist of two joints of marijuana millions of genitals an unpublishable private literature that jetplanes 1400 miles an hour and twentyfive-thousand mental institutions.

I say nothing about my prisons nor the millions of underprivileged who live in my flowerpots under the light of five hundred suns.

I have abolished the whorehouses of France, Tangiers is the next to go.

My ambition is to be President despite the fact that I'm a Catholic.

America how can I write a holy litany in your silly mood?

I will continue like Henry Ford my strophes are as individual as his automobiles more so they're all different sexes.

America I will sell you strophes $2500 apiece $500 down on your old strophe

America free Tom Mooney

America save the Spanish Loyalists

America Sacco & Vanzetti must not die

America I am the Scottsboro boys.

America when I was seven momma took me to Communist Cell meetings they sold us garbanzos a handful per ticket a ticket costs a nickel and the speeches were free everybody was angelic and sentimental about the workers it was all so sincere you have no idea what a good thing the party was in 1835 Scott Nearing was a grand old man a real mensch Mother Bloor the Silk-strikers' Ewig-Weibliche made me cry I once saw the Yiddish orator Israel Amter plain. Everybody must have been a spy.

America you don't really want to go to war.

America it's them bad Russians.

Them Russians them Russians and them Chinamen. And
   them Russians.
The Russia wants to eat us alive. The Russia's power mad.
   She wants to take our cars from out our garages.
Her wants to grab Chicago. Her needs a Red *Reader's Digest*.
   Her wants our auto plants in Siberia. Him big bureau-
   cracy running our fillingstations.
That no good. Ugh. Him make Indians learn read. Him need
   big black niggers. Hah. Her make us all work sixteen
   hours a day. Help.
America this is quite serious.
America this is the impression I get from looking in the
   television set.
America is this correct?
I'd better get right down to the job.
It's true I don't want to join the Army or turn lathes in
   precision parts factories, I'm nearsighted and psycho-
   pathic anyway.
America I'm putting my queer shoulder to the wheel.

                              Berkeley, January 17, 1956

CHEZ REXROTH

In the dark
of the winter half past seven
wet feet
the high stairs
to your nine room flat.
Hallway greetings
smiles of your unraveled
black tie;
the doors opened
to the oak table
round
     effusions of
garlic and roasted lamb.

Lamplight,
     illumination of the
gas grate,
     feet multiplication
     of the wooden chairs
in the red varnished floor.

Salutations to Homer,
Catullus and Sappho
     Jonson,
          Landor,
John Donne,
          Mallarmé,

Francis Carco
and the King James
          version.
Hail to communal beginnings
and the song of each one
in the assembly of sing.

The spell is cast
we sit down to talk
          about poetry.
Sound of ruffles,
flowered flannel shirts
Mary and Katharine,
a chain of small arms
          round your neck
The light in our faces
listening in measure
to the dimension
          of your speech
and laughter.
Syllables:
          a sigh of duration
and cut-outs in time
               and feeling.
Weight of your words
thoughts of your silence.
What was our own
          the more our own
               to speak
                    our speech,
feelings not yet
               scented.

Marthe, your very wife,
entering
          no embroidery
in her hands,
her face naked
          your heart
                    beating
on the edge of your eyelashes.

With one eye closed
               you read
     poems
Our words drifting,
the chaff binned
          with the grain.

The long ago of Sappho
makes our poetic
               horizon
                    recede:
"When they were tired
night rained her
thick dark sleep
upon their eyes."
We talk of Li Po
remember how
       he was thrown out of
               Court
"See the moon, how she glances
       responses to my song,
See my shadow, it dances
       so lightly along."

And Po Chu: "The kingfisher coverlet is chill
with none to share its warmth."
We throw bridges
                across the ages
        long ago poets
minstrels
        carriers of songs,
no creators, they
but we cannot deny
                Ezra Pound.

        Fire
        in the gas grate
heart-beats,
immediacy of perceiving
                on beat
                off beat,
and George
        walking out
                into the street
carrying his poem
        like a monstrance.

from "Autobiography"

I am leading a quiet life
in Mike's Place every day
watching the champs
of the Dante Billiard Parlor
and the French pinball addicts.
I am leading a quiet life
on lower East Broadway.
I am an American.
I was an American boy.
I read the American Boy Magazine
and became a boy scout
in the suburbs.
I thought I was Tom Sawyer
catching crayfish in the Bronx River
and imagining the Mississippi.
I had a baseball mit
and an American Flyer bike.
I delivered the Woman's Home Companion
at five in the afternoon
or the Herald Trib
at five in the morning.
I still can hear the paper thump
on lost porches.
I had an unhappy childhood.
I saw Lindberg land.
I looked homeward
and saw no angel.

I got caught stealing pencils
from the Five and Ten Cent Store
the same month I made Eagle Scout.
I chopped trees for the CCC
and sat on them.
I landed in Normandy
in a rowboat that turned over.
I have seen the educated armies
on the beach at Dover.
I have seen Egyptian pilots in purple clouds'
shopkeepers rolling up their blinds
at midday
potato salad and dandelions
at anarchist picnics.
I am reading "Lorna Doone"
and a life of John Most
terror of the industrialist
a bomb on his desk at all times.
I have seen the garbagemen parade
in the Columbus Day Parade
behind the glib
farting trumpeters.
I have not been out to the Cloisters
in a long time
nor to the Tuileries
but I still keep thinking
of going.
I have seen the garbagemen parade
when it was snowing.
I have eaten hotdogs in ballparks.
I have heard the Gettysburg Address
and the Ginsberg Address.

I like it here
and I won't go back
where I came from.
I too have ridden boxcars boxcars boxcars.
I have travelled among unknown men.
I have been in Asia
with Noah in the Ark.
I was in India
when Rome was built.
I have been in the Manger
with an Ass.
I have seen the Eternal Distributor
from a White Hill
in South San Francisco
and the Laughing Woman at Loona Park
outside the Fun House
in a great rainstorm
still laughing.
I have heard the sound of revelry
by night.
I have wandered lonely
as a crowd.
I am leading a quiet life
outside of Mike's Place every day
watching the world walk by
in its curious shoes.

[IT IS LONELY]

It is lonely

I must draw water from the well   75 buckets for the bath
I mix a drink—gin, fizz water, lemon juice, a spoonful
of strawberry jam

And place it in a champagne glass—it is hard work
to make the bath

And my winter clothes are dusty and should be put away

In storage.   Have I lost all values I wonder
the world is slippery to hold on to

When you begin to deny it.

Outside outside are the crickets and frogs in the rice fields

Large black butterflies like birds.

THE BAGEL SHOP JAZZ

Shadow people, projected on coffee shop walls
Memory formed echoes of a generation past,
Beating into now.

Nightfall creatures, eating each other,
Over a noisy cup of coffee.

Mulberry-eyed girls, in black stockings,
Smelling vaguely of mint jelly,
Making profound remarks on the shapes of navels,
Wondering how the short Sunset week
Became the long Grant Avenue night.
Love-tinted, beat angels,
Doomed to see their coffee dreams
Crushed on the floors of time,
As they fling their arrow-legs
To the heavens,
Losing their doubts in the beat.

Turtle-neck angel guys, black haired dungaree guys,
Caesar-jawed, with synagogue eyes,
World travelers, on the forty-one bus,
Mixing jazz with paint talk,
High rent, Bartok, classical murders,
The pot shortage, and last night's bust.
Lost in a dream world,
Where time is told with a beat.

Coffee-faced Ivy-Leaguers, in Cambridge jackets,
Whose personal Harvard was a Fillmore district step,
Weighted down with Conga drums,
The ancestral cross, the Othello laid curse,
Talking of Bird, Diz and Miles,
The secret, terrible hurts,
Wrapped in cool hipster smiles,
Telling themselves under the talk,
This shot must be the end,
Hoping the beat is really the truth.

The guilty police arrive.

Brief, beautiful shadows, burned on the wall of night.

A SUDDEN SKETCH POEM

Gary's sink has a shroudy burlap
  the rub brush tinware plout
    leans on right side
    like a red woman's hair
  the faucet leaks like lovedrops
The teacup's upsidedown with visions
  of green mountains and brown lousy
  Chinese mysterious up heights
  The frying pan's still wet
  The spoon's by 2 petals of flower
  The washrag's hung on edge like bloomers
I dont know what to say
    about the dishpan, the soap
  The sink itself inside or what
  is hidden underneath the bomb burlap
Shroudflap except two onions
  And an orange and old wheat germ.
Wheat meal. The hoodlatch heliograph
With the cross that makes the devil
Hiss, ah, the upper coral sensen soups
  And fast condiments, curries, rices,
Roaches, reels, tin, tip, plastickets,
  Toothbrushes and armies, and armies
Of insulated schiller, squozen gumbrop
  Peste pans, light of marin, pirshyar,
Magic dancing lights of gray and white
And all for verse I wrote it

April 1956, McCorkle's Shack

MILTON BY FIRELIGHT

"O hell, what do mine eyes
                with grief behold?"
Working with an old
Singlejack miner, who can sense
The vein and cleavage
In the very guts of rock, can
Blast granite, build
Switchbacks that last for years
Under the beat of snow, thaw, mule-hooves.
What use, Milton, a silly story
Of our lost general parents,
                eaters of fruit?

The Indian, the chainsaw boy,
And a string of six mules
Came riding down to camp
Hungry for tomatoes and green apples.
Sleeping in saddle-blankets
Under a bright night-sky
Han River slantwise by morning.
Jays squall
Coffee boils

In ten thousand years the Sierras
Will be dry and dead, home of the scorpion.
Ice-scratched slabs and bent trees.
No paradise, no fall,

Only the weathering land
The wheeling sky,
Man, with his Satan
Scouring the chaos of the mind.
Oh Hell!

Fire down
Too dark to read, miles from a road
The bell-mare clangs in the meadow
That packed dirt for a fill-in
Scrambling through loose rocks
On an old trail
All of a summer's day.

Piute Creek, August 1955

THE LATE SNOW & LUMBER STRIKE
OF THE SUMMER OF FIFTY-FOUR

Whole towns shut down
    hitching the Coast road, only gypos
Running their beat trucks, no logs on
Gave me rides. Loggers all gone fishing
Chainsaws in a pool of cold oil
On back porches of ten thousand
Split-shake houses, quiet in summer rain.
Hitched north all of Washington
Crossing and re-crossing the passes
Blown like dust, no place to work.

Climbing the steep ridge below Shuksan
    clumps of pine
    float out the fog
No place to think or work
    drifting.

On Mt. Baker, alone
In a gully of blazing snow:
Cities down the long valleys west
Thinking of work, but here,
Burning in sun-glare
Below a wet cliff, above a frozen lake,
The whole Northwest on strike
Black burners cold,
The green-chain still,

I must turn and go back:
    caught on a snowpeak
    between heaven and earth
And stand in lines in Seattle.
Looking for work.

HYMNUS AD PATREM SINENSIS

I praise those ancient Chinamen
Who left me a few words,
Usually a pointless joke or a silly question
A line of poetry drunkenly scrawled on the margin of a quick
        splashed picture—bug, leaf,
          caricature of Teacher
    on paper held together now by little more than ink
    & their own strength brushed momentarily over it
Their world & several others since
Gone to hell in a handbasket, they knew it—
Cheered as it whizzed by—
& conked out among the busted spring rain cherryblossom
    winejars
Happy to have saved us all.

31:viii:58

FOR C.

I wanted to bring you this Jap iris
Orchid-white with yellow blazons
But I couldn't face carrying it down the street
Afraid everyone would laugh
And now they're dying of my cowardice.

Abstract beauty in the garden
In my hand, in the street it is a sign
A whole procession of ithyphallic satyrs
Through a town whose people like to believe:
"I was made like Jesus, out of Love; my daddy was a spook."

The upright flower would scare them. "What's shot,"
They think, "From the big flesh cannon will decay."
Not being there I can't say that being born is a chance
To learn, to love and to save each other from ourselves:
Live ignorance rots us worse than any grave.

And lacking the courage to tell you, "I'm here,
Such as I am; I need you and you need me"
Planning to give you this flower instead—
Intending it to mean "This is really I, tall, slender,
Perfectly formed"—is uglier than their holy fantasies,

Worse to look at than my own gross shape.
After all this fuss about flowers I walked out
Just to walk, not going to see you (I had nothing to bring—
This poem wasn't finished, didn't say
What was on my mind; I'd given up)

I saw bushes of crimson rhododendron, sparkling wet
Beside the hospital walk—I had to see you.
If you were out, I'd leave these flowers.
Even if I couldn't write or speak
At least I broke and stole that branch with love.

Berkeley 16:iv:57

FOR MY FATHER

Being a modest man, you wanted
Expected an ordinary child
And here's this large, inscrutable object

ME

(Buddha's mother only dreamed
of a white elephant;
my mother . . .)

Cross between a TV camera and a rotary press
Busy turning itself into many printed pages
Heavy, a dust-collector, almost impossible
to get off your hands, out of your house
Whatever it was, not an actual child

You recognize parts of the works, ones you first donated
But what are they doing—the flywheel horizontal
Spinning two directions at once
A walking-beam connected to a gear train turning cam-
shafts—
Which produces material like this
Sometimes worth money to folks in New York
Or not, nobody knows why.

[NOT YET 40, MY BEARD IS ALREADY WHITE.]

Not yet 40, my beard is already white.
Not yet awake, my eyes are puffy and red,
　　　　like a child who has cried too much.

What is more disagreeable
than last night's wine?

I'll shave.
I'll stick my head in the cold spring and
look around at the pebbles.
Maybe I can eat a can of peaches.

Then I can finish the rest of the wine,
write poems till I'm drunk again,
and when the afternoon breeze comes up

I'll sleep until I see the moon
and the dark trees
and the nibbling deer

and hear
the quarreling coons

A SUPERMARKET IN CALIFORNIA

What thoughts I have of you tonight, Walt Whitman, for I walked down the sidestreets under the trees with a headache self-conscious looking at the full moon.

In my hungry fatigue, and shopping for images, I went into the neon fruit supermarket, dreaming of your enumerations!

What peaches and what penumbras! Whole families shopping at night! Aisles full of husbands! Wives in the avocados, babies in the tomatoes!—and you, García Lorca, what were you doing down by the watermelons?

I saw you, Walt Whitman, childless, lonely old grubber, poking among the meats in the refrigerator and eyeing the grocery boys.

I heard you asking questions of each: Who killed the pork chops? What price bananas? Are you my Angel?

I wandered in and out of the brilliant stacks of cans following you, and followed in my imagination by the store detective.

We strode down the open corridors together in our solitary fancy tasting artichokes, possessing every frozen delicacy, and never passing the cashier.

Where are we going, Walt Whitman? The doors close in an hour. Which way does your beard point tonight?

(I touch your book and dream of our odyssey in the supermarket and feel absurd.)

Will we walk all night through solitary streets? The trees add shade to shade, lights out in the houses, we'll both be lonely.

Will we stroll dreaming of the lost America of love past blue automobiles in driveways, home to our silent cottage?

Ah, dear father, graybeard, lonely old courage-teacher, what America did you have when Charon quit poling his ferry and you got out on a smoking bank and stood watching the boat disappear on the black waters of Lethe?

Berkeley, 1955

THE RUG

I'd draw all this into a fine element,—a color.
Rosy, rust-red, Orange white.

It's love; I bring it, hair-on-end.
A reflection in my eyes—part of this still room,

our strange shape—and I put my hands

to you—like cool jazz coming.
Seeing these designs we make in pure air.
I'm half-man, half-snake—and you
A BURROW
There are no words but color and muscled form
AND THIS IS NOT IT
I can't remember that instant
and I alter it to elegance
to flowers and animals—and no speech
covers the blankness.
I'm filled perfectly, giving your gift to me.
AND THIS IS NOT IT
This is failure, no trick, no end
but speech for those who'll listen.
I cry "Love, Love, Love, Love Love,"
but this is not my voice—
these are enormous forms
Rosy, rust-red, Orange, white!

POINT LOBOS: ANIMISM

It is possible my friend,
If I have had a fat belly
That the wolf lives on fat
Gnawing slowly
Through a visceral night of rancor.
It is possible that the absence of pain
May be so great
That the possibility of care
May be impossible.

Perhaps to know pain.
Anxiety, rather than the fear
Of the fear of anxiety.
This talk of miracles!

Of Animism:
I have been in a spot so full of spirits
That even the most joyful animist
Brooded
When all in sight was less to be cared about
Than death
And there was no noise in the ears
That mattered.
(I knelt in the shade
By a cold salt pool
And felt the entrance of hate
On many legs,
The soul like a clambering
Water vascular system.

No scuttling could matter
Yet I formed in my mind
The most beautiful
Of maxims.
How could I care
For your illness or mine?)
This talk of bodies!

It is impossible to speak
Of lupine or tulips
When one may read
His name
Spelled by the mold on the stumps
When the forest moves about one.
Heel. Nostril.
Light. Light! Light!
This is the bird's song
You may tell it
to your children.

joes song

once upon
and eversince
i was a child
in a childs world

i have wept a childs tears
and built a childs wall
of clay and stone
and colored years
of poems in paint
and virgins gold

i sought to build
a wall so tall
of lion eggs
from galilee
a brick of song
among the dregs
of silver nails
and lesser men
—a mile long
to kiss the sun
and climb again

once ago
and ever now
i stood a man
on a childs wall

i stopped and prayed
to spiderwebs
and roses of the sea
i spoke as one
with all the earth
and knew the pain
of birth and death
to be the same
without my wall

once upon
and everfurled
i stand alone
with all the world

IN TRANSIT

Question: Locate the center of infinity
Answer: Anywhere
IT   NEVER   STOPS   MOVING!

The ceaseless alchemical permutation, gold into history,
rain into strawberries, strawberries into my bloodstream,
my blood into flowering dreams

the dream into absolute perception, into coruscating
        visions of
THIS IS WHERE IT IS BA–BY into
infinity

It is necessary to search the spirit through the light of one's
own bioluminescence

THERE IS NO SUCH THING AS STANDING STILL

The balance is that of a gyroscope, motion existing within
        motion
the balance of a bird listening to its heartbeat
wings poised against the currents of the air, eyes tracing the
turning of the earth, the planet circling the sun, the sun
        spinning
its golden path in the universe, and the universe breeding
        life and
death in infinity

and the bird hangs halfway up the sky
infinite motion   at rest   within infinite motion

LET IT GO!

"Whatever you see that is beautiful
        don't hang on to it
whatever you see that is terrible
        don't hang on to it"

LET IT GO!

The balance is that of sunlight on water
the sunlight is moving as the earth turns, the water
following its gravity path into eventual raindrops
and home to another river
the sunlight-and-water being one and together for the
        duration
of their parallel flow

there is no way to stop water
if you lock it up it will evaporate and reach the clouds
        anyhow
there is no way to stop the sun
it holds its own galactic balance and moves
according to the nebulae of outer space

LET IT GO!

IT NEVER STOPS MOVING

there is movement within a mountain
a rock, a thought, a flower, a light bulb,
a cat, a star, a rice bowl, an arrow

LET IT GO!

IT NEVER STOPS MOVING

there is no such thing as standing still
the direction of motion is frequently a matter of choice
when you try to stop other things from moving
you give yourself an impetus toward backwards motion

LET IT GO!

Most of the time
  you will be the *it*
being let go of

SMALL PRAYER FOR FALLING ANGELS

too many of my friends are junkies
too many of my psychic kin tattoo invisible revelations on
    themselves
signing their manifestoes to etheric consciousness with little
hoofprint scars reaching from fingertip to fingertip
a gory religiosity akin to Kali's sacred necklace of fifty human
heads

Kali-Ma, Kali-Mother; Kali-Ma, Kali-Mother
too many of my friends are running out of blood, their veins
are collapsing, it takes them half an hour to get a hit
their blood whispers through their bodies, singing its own
    death chant
in a voice of fire, in a voice of glaciers, in a voice of sand
    that blows
forever
over emptiness

Kali-Ma, remember the giving of life as well as the giving of
    death
        Kali-Ma . . .
Kali-Ma, remember the desire is for enlightenment and not
    oblivion
        Kali-Ma . . .
Kali-Ma, their bones are growing light; help them to fly
Kali-Ma, their eyes burn with the pain of fire; help them that
    they see

with clear sight
Kali-Ma, their blood sings death to them; remind them of
    life
that they be born once more
that they slide bloody through the gates of yes, that
they relax their hands nor try to stop the movement of the
    flowing now

too many of my friends have fallen into the white heat of the
    only flame
may they fly higher; may there be no end to flight

IT IS AN OUTFIELDER

for N. H.

The playground is so filled with kids
that their games overlap, the
outfielders of one game
standing on the basepaths of the opposite
diamond; running around in between.
A fat girl out in left field
is standing with her arms folded
talking to a boy while she (nervously)
adjusts her glasses.
Suddenly she turns, unfolds her arms
& catches a fly ball for the 3rd out.

SONGS FOR MOTHER & CHILD: 2

Make a kite with bamboo bracing.
Become an expert for the first time.
Don't watch the pros.
Fly it in the Park with the kids
& the old men. Gently
let the string out, feel it
tickle your hands. Watch
the sky, cluttered with shapes
of clouds & kites, accept
your kite.

With spirit, silence, joy,
watch how high your kite flies—
its string hanging like a spider thread
touched by the wind. Watch
the constant & huge clouds move
delicate & free. Release
the string & watch your kite
go higher than them all.
Become a sage for the first time.

FUD AT FOSTER'S

Bowl of cold turkie fool
A roast chicken liver louie
My cigarillo's going out in a spanish bedroom
Jazz is for free
Coke is for free
Junk's unlimited and sold by Agents
      that I can make poems that I spin the day to
      Tim Buck Two that I lose tension and head
      floats forever a far inscape of lemon trees AND
NO MORE REALITY SANDWICHES!!!

Can I ever get up from this table?
Can I ever stop thunder?
Can I make it to windows of fur?
Can I soup up her eyes in a can of star milk and shoot it for
                                             light?

Can I read in the park?
Can I sit on the Moon? Can I?
Oh stop it! Oh start! Oh, make music
Though your arm is too thin
  and the jails are too small, sweaty AND STINK!

THE DISLOCATED HIPSTER

When Gabriel was practicing the other day,
    making few riffs for kicks
    (and in preparation for the day
when there'd be just that one cool sound
    in all the world, and
when everyone would swing with it),
    the other boys in the group
    were backing him up fine & sweet
    with that new happy kind of jazz.

Well, when Gabriel had made his bit
    he backed off neat
and the tenor man started
    making it like Eden before apples,
I mean he was blowing clean air
    all over the place.

And the air got so clear
    it was a natural high
    just to breathe it,
and that man was breathing it
    straight from the mouth of God.

And he was floating in a yard off the stand
by the time he'd made his chorus
and so when he got down
and the man in the back

started making the mallets,
why, he took the plunge
right off that stand
    and he fell, man
arms and legs and axe and all
went flying through that cool air
and it was a crazy scene.

And he landed right in the middle
    of Grant Avenue last night
and this scene hasn't been at all the same since then:

    The bells in all the towers have been ringing
    and the sun kept shining all night
    and the pigeons are still up there in the topaz sky
    and the flowers are on overtime pushing sweet smells
    and people are dancing in the streets
    and man, everything is swinging and joyous
    and the light in everyone's eyes is just too much

because when that tenor man starts blowing
    each time it gets around to him
they really dig that dislocated hipster . . .
                            the most!

HOW MANY BIG THINGS

How many big things
　　can you name on your fingers
　　　little things

a star perhaps; a star
　　is small if a kiss is
　　　a rose

or have you listened to
　　brooks' often words talking
　　　to pebbles

(and hear soft whispers walking
　　in your own ear when
　　　she is)

a wanton air in many leaves
　　rustling their skirts with
　　　wind lips

or fingers of grass, green
　　sun, and much too soft for
　　　flowers' rings

the dark frown of mountains
　　more breathless and white than
　　　doves' breasts

(dare to touch the tips
   of the rising smiles of her
      eyes' lips)

or a fog a bee's mouth, gray,
   while wrapping itself around
      sad places

if a face is seen before
   the billows of ships' sails in
      a cloud

then the tip-toe cotton of children's
   feet is the torrents and winds
      of rains

(o how many big things
   if she loves you in little
      many ways)

[MY FATHER DIED THIS SPRING]

My father died this spring
      Well, I had meant to write more often
To a kind of hell it must be, with all unresolved difficulties.
      I had greens with vinegar last night—that's something
in common
        And I would have told him that—adding it
      to a list of possible conversations
With the pictures on his dressing table
      of all his daughters
but he wasn't flinging out his arms to keep a soul there.
        You can't say he wasn't strange
      and difficult.
        How far does one go
   to help a parent like a child—when he waits
    at the employees entrance in old clothes
        and I don't want him.
        Well he'll be there waiting
for me. Demands just, wanted, or not
      are to be met.
And let me see, yes the demon large
      impossible and yields without vanishing
  no power, no satisfaction
       sitting on the back porch drinking beer
       following me to the sick squirrels in the cellar.
And the material things, calling cards
    engraved watches, trunks that married life brings
      full of stuff

he left behind 10 years ago.   The golf clubs.   The fact is
   there was a man, a married man,
  and an old man.   it's impossible to know.
    but blood does bring curiosity.

9.15.63

REVOLUTIONARY LETTERS

(dedicated to Bob Dylan)

29
beware of those
who say we are the beautiful losers
who stand in their long hair and wait to be punished
who weep on beaches for our isolation

we are not alone: we have brothers in all the hills
we have sisters in the jungles and in the ozarks
we even have brothers on the frozen tundra
they sit by their fires, they sing, they gather arms
they multiply: they will reclaim the earth

nowhere we can go but they are waiting for us
no exile where we will not hear welcome home
"goodmorning brother, let me work with you
goodmorning sister, let me
fight by your side"

LIFE CHANT

> *may it come that all the radiances*
> *will be known as our own radiance*
> —Tibetan Book of the Dead

cacophony of small birds at dawn
        may it continue
sticky monkey flowers on bare brown hills
        may it continue
bitter taste of early miner's lettuce
        may it continue
music on city streets in the summer nights
        may it continue
kids laughing on roofs on stoops on the beach in the snow
        may it continue
triumphal shout of the newborn
        may it continue
deep silence of great rainforests
        may it continue
fine austerity of jungle peoples
        may it continue
rolling fuck of great whales in turquoise ocean
        may it continue
clumsy splash of pelican in smooth bays
        may it continue
astonished human eyeball squinting thru aeons at astonished
                                   nebulae who squint back
        may it continue

clean snow on the mountain
      may it continue
fierce eyes, clear light of the aged
      may it continue
rite of birth & of naming
      may it continue
rite of instruction
      may it continue
rite of passage
      may it continue
love in the morning, love in the noon sun
love in the evening among crickets
      may it continue
long tales by fire, by window, in fog, in dusk on the mesa
      may it continue
love in thick midnight, fierce joy of old ones loving
      may it continue
the night music
      may it continue
grunt of mating hippo, giraffe, foreplay of snow leopard
             screeching of cats on the backyard
             fence
      may it continue
without police
      may it continue
without prisons
      may it continue
without hospitals, death medicine: flu & flu vaccine
      may it continue
without madhouses, marriage, highschools that are prisons
      may it continue
without empire
      may it continue

in sisterhood
        may it continue
thru the wars to come
        may it continue
in brotherhood
        may it continue
tho the earth seem lost
        may it continue
thru exile & silence
        may it continue
with cunning & love
        may it continue
as woman continues
        may it continue
as breath continues
        may it continue
as stars continue
        may it continue

    may the wind kindly w/us
    may the fire remember our names
    may springs flow, rain fall again
    may the land grow green, may it swallow our mistakes

we begin to work
        may it continue
the great transmutation
        may it continue
a new heaven & a new earth
        may it continue
        may it continue

from *NOTES OF A DIRTY OLD MAN*

I met Kerouac's boy Neal C. shortly before he went down to lay along those Mexican railroad tracks to die. his eyes were sticking out on ye old toothpicks and he had his head in the speaker, jogging, bouncing, ogling, he was in a white t-shirt and seemed to be singing like a cuckoo bird along with the music, *preceding* the beat just a shade as if he were leading the parade. I sat down with my beer and watched him. I'd brought in a six pack or two. Bryan was handing out an assignment and some film to two young guys who were going to cover that show that kept getting busted. [Michael McClure's play *The Beard*] whatever happened to that show by the Frisco poet, I forget his name. anyhow, nobody was noticing Neal C. and Neal C. didn't care, or he pretended not to. when the song stopped, the 2 young guys left and Bryan introduced me to the fab. Neal C.

"have a beer?" I asked him.

Neal plucked a bottle out, tossed it in the air, caught it, ripped the cap off and emptied the half-quart in two long swallows.

"have another."

"sure."

"I thought I was good on the beer."

"I'm the tough young jail kid. I've read your stuff."

"read your stuff too. that bit about climbing out the bathroom window and hiding in the bushes naked. good stuff."

"oh yeah." he worked at the beer. he never sat down. he kept moving around the floor. he was a little punchy with the action, the eternal light, but there wasn't any hatred in him. you liked him even though you didn't want to because Kerouac had set him up for the sucker punch and Neal had bit, kept biting. but you know Neal was o.k. and another way of looking at it, Jack had only written the book, he wasn't Neal's mother. just his destructor, deliberate or otherwise. Neal was dancing around the room on the Eternal High. his face looked old, pained, all that, but his body was the body of a boy of eighteen.

"you want to try him, Bukowski?" asked Bryan.

"yeah, ya wanta go, baby?" he asked me.

again, no hatred. just going with the game.

"no, thanks. I'll be forty-eight in August. I've taken my last beating."

I couldn't have handled him.

"when was the last time you saw Kerouac?" I asked.

I think he said 1962, 1963. anyhow, a long time back.

I just about stayed with Neal on the beer and had to go out and get some more. the work at the office was about done and Neal was staying at Bryan's and B. invited me over for dinner. I said, "all right," and being a bit high I didn't realize what was going to happen.

when we got outside a very light rain was just beginning to fall. the kind that really fucks up the streets. I still didn't know. I thought Bryan was going to drive. but Neal got in and took the wheel. I had the back seat anyhow. B. got up in front with Neal. and the ride began. straight along those slippery streets and it would seem we were past the corner and then Neal would decide to take a right or a left. past parked cars, the dividing line just a hair away. it can only be described as hairline. a tick the other way and we were all finished.

after we cleared I would always say something ridiculous like, "well, suck my dick!" and Bryan would laugh and Neal would just go on driving, neither grim or happy or sardonic, just there—doing the movements. I understood. it was necessary. it was his bull ring, his racetrack. it was *holy* and necessary.

the best one was just off Sunset, going north toward Carlton. the drizzle was good now, ruining both the vision and the streets. turning off of Sunset, Neal picked up his next move, full-speed chess, it had to be calculated in an instant's glance. a left on Carlton would bring us to Bryan's. we were a block off. there was one car ahead of us and two approaching. now, he could have slowed down and followed the traffic in but he would have lost his *movement*. not Neal. he swung out around the car ahead of us and I thought, this is it, well, it doesn't matter, really it doesn't matter at all. that's the way it goes through your brain, that's the way it went through my brain. the two cars plunged at each other, head-on, the other so close that the headlights flooded my back seat. I do think that at the last second the other driver touched his brake. that gave us the hairline. it must have been figured in by Neal. that movement. but it wasn't over. we were going very high speed now and the other car, approaching slowly from Hollywood Blvd. was just about blocking a left on Carlton. I'll always remember the color of that car. we got that close. a kind of gray-blue, an old car, coupe, humped and hard like a rolling steel brick thing. Neal cut left. to me it looked as if we were going to ram right through the center of the car. it was obvious. but somehow, the motion of the other car's forward and our movement left coincided perfectly. the hairline was there. once again. Neal parked the thing and we went on in. Joan brought the dinner in.

Neal ate all of his plate and most of mine too. we had a bit of wine. John had a highly intelligent young homosexual baby-sitter, who I now think has gone on with some rock band or killed himself or something. anyhow, I pinched his buttocks as he walked by. he loved it.

I think I stayed long past my time, drinking and talking with Neal. the baby-sitter kept talking about Hemingway, somehow equating me with Hemingway until I told him to shove it and he went upstairs to check Jason. it was a few days later that Bryan phoned me:

"Neal's dead, Neal died."

"oh shit, no."

then Bryan told me something about it. hung up.

that was it.

all those rides, all those pages of Kerouac, all that jail, to die alone under a frozen Mexican moon, alone, you understand? can't you see the miserable puny cactii? Mexico is not a bad place because it is simply oppressed; Mexico is simply a bad place. can't you see the desert animals watching? the frogs, horned and simple, the snakes like slits of men's minds crawling, stopping, waiting, dumb under a dumb Mexican moon. reptiles, flicks of things, looking across this guy in the sand in a white t-shirt.

Neal, he's found his movement, hurt nobody. the tough young jail kid laying it down alongside a Mexican railroad track.

the only night I met him I said, "Kerouac has written all your other chapters. I've already written your last one."

"go ahead," he said, "write it."

end copy.

from **THE FRISCO KID**

To know America you've got to stand in the middle of the Golden Gate Bridge. You haven't experienced America, the sheer obscene power of her, until you've stood in the middle of the Golden Gate Bridge and listened to its roar. The Brooklyn Bridge won't do, nor will any of those other Hart Crane bridges back on the worn-out Eastern shore; they're part of another time, another epoch, really, and the songs they sing are not the songs I sing. That America is another country, a country gone like the water that flows through the Golden Gate in San Francisco. The Golden Gate Bridge is the new America! It is the new America risen out of the ashes of the old, an America tottering on the edge of the apocalypse, so wild, so insane, so intense, frenetic, schizophrenic, per-verted, fucked-up, and Free! that all the angels—San Fran-cisco angels—open their wings in delight and deliver themselves, *are themselves,* when they discover that magical flight! The Golden Gate Bridge is the new America in all its tensile strength, two hundred million people hacking and scraping and swabbing at the flecks of rust showing through, spreading paint over the cracks and creaks and hidden flaws, wrapping their own lives around the stresses and strains that are invisible to the ordinary tourist. The Golden Gate Bridge is the shivering wind-whipped wand connecting two worlds: the old one of pastoral peace and old men in back-country shoes, and the new one of highstepping young sons who march off their time in dreams and songs and endless vistas.

Frankie jumped off the Golden Gate Bridge yesterday. We bury her tomorrow.

. . .

Whenever I go to the park, I stop by and see Shoeshine Devine. Shoeshine Devine lives in the San Gottardo Hotel in North Beach, but during the day he likes to hang out around the children's playground in Golden Gate Park. He goes up to old Italian grandfathers who are babysitting on the benches and thrusts his shoeshine box under their noses and says, "D'you want a shine?" Sometimes one of the old men nods and Shoeshine Devine squats down in front of him—he doesn't use a stool—he squats on his haunches and bounces up and down as he spits and polishes the old man's fifty-year-old shoes, carefully cleaning and polishing around each hook and eye. More often than not, though, the old men say no, and Shoeshine Devine strides through the playground with his box clutched under his arm, moving among the swings and slides and benches like a spectral ghost, his gaunt jaw thrust forward, pausing occasionally to give a swing a push or lift a kid out of the sand. Sometimes he stands still among the children's playthings with a look in his eye that seems to pierce the metal of the swings. The kids like Shoeshine Devine, but occasionally an old Sicilian grandmother snatches her charge out of his line of vision, hustling across to the other side of the playground, where they stay until he leaves.

The box Shoeshine Devine carries under his arm was custom built for him by Mr. Hum who owns a restaurant on Washington Street in Chinatown. This was when Shoeshine Devine was just emerging from his hallucinatory period and was still called Johnny Woodrose. What happened was, when Johnny was coming out of his hallucinatory period he started hanging aroung Mr. Hum's restaurant. The restaurant is famous among the drifters and wine-drinkers of North Beach because of its cheap food. Mr. Hum and all the Hum relatives work in the back of the restaurant making pork rolls and steamed rice. Johnny could buy a pork roll and a bowl of steamed rice for twenty cents. That's a pretty cheap feed in anybody's restaurant. Then, maybe because of Johnny's fading hallucinations, Mr. Hum started giving him his pork roll and bowl of steamed rice for free. One day while Johnny was eating his free food, Mr. Hum said, "You rant crean table?" Johnny said, "Sure," and started to clean Mr. Hum's tables. After a few months Mr. Hum approached Johnny again and said, "You rant eat black loom?" Johnny started eating in the back room with Mr. Hum and all the other Hums. When Johnny told me about Mr. Hum, he said, "I have never seen such translucent hands."

"What do you mean?"

"Looking at Mr. Hum's hands is like looking through the transparent membrane of a fish."

I was interested in what Johnny said, so I went to the restaurant one evening and looked at Mr. Hum's hands. Johnny was right.

After working in the restaurant for six months, Mr. Hum called Johnny into the back room. "You rant to rearn tlade?" he asked.

Johnny shrugged. At the time, he was following the path of least resistance and he looked upon Mr. Hum as sort of a Buddhahead. "There are things the Chinese know that we haven't even started to think about, Kid. I think that all those guys who are standing on their heads and trying to Zen it through should go see Mr. Hum. He's already there. He's standing on his head."

Mr. Hum made Johnny a shoeshine box. Johnny looked upon the shoeshine box as a mystical talisman, a sign that he should go among the multitudes and shine their shoes, always giving a good shine for fifteen cents. "This shoeshine box is bigger than the Bank of America, Kid. I don't want any more or less than fifteen cents per shine."

One day in Union Square a customer took a felt-tipped pen and wrote "Shoeshine Devine" on the side of his box. Johnny took this as further proof of his calling, so he changed his name to Shoeshine Devine and started keeping a journal. He called it *The Journal of Shoeshine Devine: The Will and Testament of an American Shoeshine Boy.* He kept it in a lined notebook on whose cover was an elaborate illustration of his shoeshine box. Inside, on the first page, was the title, and on the dedication page it said, "This is to testify that Shoeshine Devine is a good shoeshine boy." Underneath that dedication were the names of one hundred and fifteen satisfied customers.

On the corner of Grant and Green I ran into Crazy Alex. Seeing him made me feel better. I automatically reached into my pocket for some change as I approached him. By day Crazy Alex sits at a corner table in the Bagel Shop and at night he stands under the awning of Ken's Grocery Store, black, thin, adept with words, passing sentence on passersby with his prosonomasia. A hundred folk tales had blossomed around Crazy Alex. One was that he was a talented painter and sculptor, living in Ajijic, Mexico, with his white wife and baby daughter when one day his wife walked into Lake Chapala and never came out. The Mexican authorities took his daughter away and Alex cracked up.

Another tale was that he had an advanced case of syphilis of the brain, that it caused the accelerated pace of his flights of verbal imagination that astounded anyone who stopped long enough to listen. Crazy Alex never stopped talking. I mean, literally, in any twenty-four-hour period you would never, not ever, hear Crazy Alex silent. Occasionally a verbal wiseacre like the world debating champion from Stanford or Cal who'd heard of Crazy Alex's ability would come over to the Beach to test his wit, you know, catch one of Crazy Alex's jibes and toss it back at him, sort of a duel of words, as it were. Catching Crazy Alex verbally was like standing under Niagara Falls and trying to stop the flow with your tongue. At first I got no sense out of Crazy Alex; his talk was too fast, too bizarre, too unrelated. Crazy Alex speaks in magnified puns and symbols.

Then one day in the middle of a twenty-four-hour monologue I suddenly realized that Crazy Alex was talking about me! I was speeding myself, having dropped half a dozen bennies the night before, and I suddenly saw that Crazy Alex was describing my life, my face, and my problems as he sat at the table. I was sitting in the Bagel Shop feeding him beers. He didn't look at me as he talked, just gazed out the window and spoke, incredibly fast, his mustache flecked with beer, his hands moving from mouth to glass to collar to table like a flight of skittery birds, and all the time his voice spewing out words in a sort of discordant rhyme that after a while assumed the rhythm of a litany, like "Yeah the light's all right if you're lookin' for light but you gotta see the night all right the sunshine's fine if you gotta dime buy the other side of the road if the road's for rent coffee ain't gonna help you if you ain't got beans know what I mean no beans no means no sunshine no funtime and keep uptight if your bread's all spent and turn on the radio no news is news all you gotta do is listen to the chime keep the soles on your shoes and watch out for screws hey baby times right for a dime c'mon it's mine if it's yours and you gottem all the time fine fine and don't pay unless you get a receipt good forever get you in all the doors even under the floors right so if you're afraid to get laid get on top and don't let it drop you can't walk the streets without being beat all reet and watch out for the heat cause if you ain't neat it's not the streetmeat you want to repeat all right it's all right baby so long's you come along and sing the proper song right or wrong ding dong hurry hurry now it's time give me a dime . . ."

I often imagine that if Crazy Alex were taped and the recording played backwards or at a different speed, everything would add up. Sometimes when I hear Crazy Alex talking, I feel his cracked brain holds all the answers, the ones Einstein missed, Fermi never knew, Newton and Heidegger and all those other cats just street-corner sitters without a Bagel Shop; Crazy Alex is the one, sitting at his table or standing underneath the awning of Ken's Grocery Store burdened with his gift of tongues, waiting for humanity to catch up with its gift of ears.

Crazy Alex spends half of his time in Agnew State Hospital and the other half on the Beach. When I asked him about Agnew, he said it was okay, only they played the radio all the time. "I know," I said. "It's terrible when they play the radio twenty-four hours a day."

"Hey, baby, that ain't the way. Where I come from, they play it twenty-five hours a day," he said.

When I walk through the streets of San Francisco, I look about me; the image is there for my eyes. It is heartrending. I am a tracer of these corners. I have stood on every one. The magic is a magic of numbers, numbers enclosed in years, in lives and lives aborted. As I walk, I try to picture who I am, what chronicle I keep. It is *The Journal of Anxiety's Child*. It is *the* book! And when I walk down Grant Avenue and see the loungers outside the Co-Existence Bagel Shop, I do not see loungers, I see poets and philosophers and children of the new age. And when I walk past the Amp Palace and see Hube the Cube and Monte and Little Joe and Joe DeLucca and Ella and Paddy O'Sullivan, I do not see these people, I see mythological creatures from another time, from another epoch really, biding time, creating out of time a new solstice that will be both the first and last day of winter. When I walk down these streets and cross Washington Square, I am transfixed by the pathos and beauty of the event, the magicalness of the hour, the incredible surrealistic ecstasy of the moment. Time is surely a stream, and that voyage begun decades ago continues, recorded here, plagiarized and copied, imprinted and embedded, Xeroxed and stamped into each vortex of my brain. It is the image of a time and America I know nothing of; it is *my* America, timewracked and weary, straddling a fault that runs compass-perfect down to the deepest reaches of the human heart. How many of us have tried to pin her down? How many of us have hung our specimens on the wall and stood back, gazing transfixed? And when I write this down, I think, Is my America your America? Do you walk these same streets? You were beside me; did you see what I saw? Where were you when I walked across the park? Did you spend your afternoons at the Colton Public Library? Did you listen to what Crazy Alex said at his corner table? Is your alley my alley? What graffiti did you read as a child? I want to know that poetry.

I am trying to recreate the sounds of my childhood. I am trying to inscribe upon the head of a pin the entire history of a unique race—a race unique because it is so maligned, so egalitarian, so democratic, so perverse, so unimaginable that the pin itself must be withdrawn from the heart, the blood wiped off, the surface burnished, cleansed with a thousand incredible romances, a million walks, countless heartbreaks, recollections, and regrets. I am trying to describe the history of something I knew, make tangible a race, an idea conceived extraterrestrially, on the moon, in the farthest reaches of space! I am trying to set down the first blueprints for the age of rebellion, that heartless, unregenerative task of making memory ring true. When I look out of my Roach Alley windows I see the entire history of my race inscribed on the head of a pin. The pin is a point. The point is embedded in my veins, the veins of my childhood. What I see is the sweeping arc of a bridge, a city that doesn't exist, a race of men monstrous in their duplicity, a girl suspended like time between bridge and water.

The Contributors

AMIRI BARAKA (LeRoi Jones until 1968). Poet, music critic, essayist, dramatist, novelist, and—after his Beat period—political activist. With Hettie Cohen (to whom he was married until 1965) he began *Yūgen* magazine (1958–62) and Totem Press. In 1961 he and Diane di Prima founded *Floating Bear*, an underground newsletter for poets.

CHARLES BUKOWSKI was born in Germany in 1920 and came to the United States at the age of three. Raised in Los Angeles, he began writing poetry when he was thirty-five years old. Bukowski regularly contributed to the underground Los Angeles newspaper *Open City*. He was the author of more than forty-five books. Charles Bukowski died on March 9, 1994.

NEAL CASSADY. Although he was not a prominent writer during the Beat period, his wild, chameleonlike personality inspired many Beat writers, including Jack Kerouac, who mythologized Cassady as Dean Moriarty in *On the Road*. His long-promised autobiography, *The First Third*, was to be published in 1963 with the help of Allen Ginsberg. However, it didn't appear until 1971, and then only as a flawed, incomplete text. City Lights Books later reissued a more accurate autobiography in the early 1980s.

GREGORY CORSO was a member of the original group of Beats that also included Jack Kerouac and Allen Ginsberg. Abandoned by his mother at age one, he lived in orphanages, foster homes, and reform schools for thirteen years—eventually making his home in the streets. Corso was largely self-educated, and began writing poetry while serving a three-year prison sentence for robbery. In 1950 he met Allen Ginsberg, who encouraged him to continue writing. Corso's first work, *The Vestal Lady on Brattle and Other Poems*, was published in 1955. Three years later, City Lights Books published *Gasoline*.

DIANE DI PRIMA. Born and raised in Brooklyn, di Prima left college in 1953 to pursue other creative interests. Her first collection of poetry, *This Kind of Bird Flies Backwards,* was published in 1958 by Hettie and LeRoi Jones's Totem Press. Di Prima is credited with founding the Poets' Press and the American Theater for Poets. Her *Selected Poems* was published by City Lights in 1990.

KENWARD ELMSLIE. A native New Yorker who later became associated with the New York School of poets, Elmslie was raised in Colorado and educated at Harvard. In addition to his numerous books of poetry, a novel, and various translations, he has written and produced six operas.

LAWRENCE FERLINGHETTI was the founder and co-owner of the first all-paperback bookstore in America, City Lights Book Shop. Located in the heart of San Francisco's North Beach, City Lights also became the name of the press that was founded soon after the bookstore opened. His Pocket Poet series published Ginsberg's *Howl* and Corso's *Gasoline*, which, along with Kerouac's *On the Road*, established the Beat Movement.

ALLEN GINSBERG. Although his work is deeply spiritual (he has for some years been a practicing Buddhist), one of his greatest attributes as a poet has been his ability to arouse and inspire young people. His nonviolent protests at demonstrations and rallies were instrumental in raising America's consciousness above its predilection for war-mongering and environmental destruction. Ginsberg is often considered the father of the Beat Generation.

TED JOANS was born on a Mississippi riverboat. From his father, a riverboat entertainer, he inherited his lifelong interest in jazz. He is also a musician and painter, and a world traveler who has placed himself in self-imposed exile, living most of every year in Africa.

LEROI JONES. *See* Amiri Baraka.

JERRY KAMSTRA. Very little is known about him aside from what he tells us in his book *The Frisco Kid*: "When I arrived in San Francisco in 1957, I discovered a community living on the edge of the city unlike any other in America. Reckless, creative, frenetic, insane, it was too insane for a lot of people—many did not survive. But I did. I came of age in the cheap pads and artists' lofts in North Beach. In the process, I lost my innocence and my youth, but gained an indelible memory of a bunch of crazy people who lived, fought, struggled, loved, and even died together with a sense of élan and community I had never experienced before nor have found since."

LENORE KANDEL moved to San Francisco in 1960, settling in the Haight-Ashbury district, where she made a living singing folk songs and playing the guitar. During this time she met and became involved with Lew Welch, who introduced her to Jack Kerouac and other Beat poets.

BOB KAUFMAN is known in France as the "American Rimbaud." An original Beat poet of the 1950s, he has been called one of the most influential black poets of his era. Kaufman joined the Merchant Marine at the age of thirteen and sailed around the world for twenty years, surviving four shipwrecks. Arriving in New York in the 1940s, he met and befriended Allen Ginsberg and William Burroughs. When John F. Kennedy was assassinated in 1963, Kaufman took a vow of silence that lasted twelve years. Some of his better-known works include *Solitudes Crowded with Loneliness* (1965), *The Golden Sardine* (1967), and, more recently, *The Ancient Rain* (1981).

JACK KEROUAC helped coin the term Beat Generation, and for much of his literary lifetime was the unofficial spokesperson of the Beats. When his work was condemned, along with the Movement, Kerouac withdrew from society and took to drinking. He died at the age of forty-seven, feeling neglected and scorned, never suspecting that he would become one of the most widely read writers of his generation. *On the Road* (1957), *The Subterraneans* (1958), and *The Dharma Bums* (1958) are his best-known works.

TULI KUPFERBERG became associated with the Beat Generation early on, adding to the mix with a great variety of artistic skills, including the establishment of his own Birth Press in

1958. He was the founder of The Fugs, an anarchist rock group that was termed "the first All-American-Skin-Rock-Peace-Sex-Psychedelic-Tenderness-Society Group" (Martin Cohen, *Avante Garde*, 1968).

JOANNE KYGER was a latecomer to the Beat scene who contributed to the second wave of the movement. She brought to American poetry the influences of Native American traditions, Buddhist scriptures, psychedelics, and certain practices of the New Age community. She was married to Gary Snyder for four years and, later, spent time in Japan and India.

PHILIP LAMANTIA considers Edgar Allen Poe to be one of his primary influences. His poetry, while more abstract and surreal than other Beat literature, has inspired countless poets, Beat and otherwise. His *Selected Poems: 1943–1966* was published in 1981 by City Lights Books.

RON LOEWINSOHN was born in the Philippines and lived there as a boy. After moving to New York, then Los Angeles, he and his family eventually settled in San Francisco, "just in time for the Beat Generation." He was barely twenty-one years old when he received an encouraging letter from the poet William Carlos Williams, which would later appear as the introduction to his first book, *Watermelons*.

WILLIAM J. MARGOLIS cofounded and coedited the first important Beat magazine, *Beatitude*, until October 1959, when he had an accident that left him a paraplegic. During this same period (beginning in 1954), he edited and published *Miscellaneous Man*, another prominent literary magazine of the period. His first book, *The Anteroom of Hell,* was published in San Francisco in 1957.

RICHARD McBRIDE wrote poems, plays, and stories while he was the business manager of City Lights Book Shop. His play *There and Where* was staged in North Beach on a double bill with William Saroyan's *Sweeney in the Trees.* He has traveled extensively and now lives in London.

MICHAEL McCLURE was one of the Beats who read his work at the famous Six Gallery poetry reading in San Francisco in 1955, the night Ginsberg gave his first public reading of *Howl.* McClure has been called a "kind of shaman-activist, cutting away at the webs of repression that in his view cripple American culture, using such traditional tools as chanting, mantras, ritual drama, music, and psychoactive drugs, and balancing himself between intensive discipline and Dionysian liberty" (Ann Charters, ed., *Dictionary of Literary Biography,* Vol. 17, p. 383).

DAVID MELTZER considers himself a "Second Generation" Beat writer. Meltzer is one of the innovators of poetry read to jazz music. He performed at the Jazz Cellar from 1957 to 1958, and later he formed a bluegrass band with his wife, Tina, which had a considerable following in North Beach, California. In addition to his many volumes of poetry, he has edited *The San Francisco Poets* (1971) and *The Secret Garden: An Anthology of Kabbalistic Texts* (1976).

PETER ORLOVSKY is perhaps more famous as the companion of Allen Ginsberg than as a poet in his own right. He began writing in 1957, after numerous requests from Ginsberg. Orlovsky has said that he carried a pen to "drop on paper like a wandering hen a green egg, observations that tickle my eye-brain or memory ear or emotional snapshots that per-kolate under my skin like a swim in November Pound . . ." (Ann Charters, ed., *Dictionary of Literary Biography*, Vol. 17, p. 435).

RON PADGETT grew up in Tulsa, Oklahoma. After reading Ginsberg's *Howl* and Kerouac's *On the Road* at the age of sixteen, he realized that he could become a writer. He is the translator of *The Complete Poems of Blaise Cendrars*, the great French proto-beatnik. His *New and Selected Poems* is forthcoming.

STUART Z. PERKOFF was often called a poet's poet, and was extremely popular in Venice West, a second major West Coast bohemian colony of the 1960s. Perkoff was "on the road" at age seventeen, spending time in New York City and on the West Coast, before settling permanently in Venice, Califor-nia. He died at the age of forty-three, just as he believed he was reaching the height of his literary career. A memorial reading of his poetry was held in Venice in 1994, on the twentieth anniversary of his death.

ED SANDERS. After reading *Howl* and *On the Road,* Ed Sand-ers left his home in Kansas for New York City with hopes of becoming a poet. His *Poem from Jail* was published in 1963, and a year later *The Toe Queen Poems*. Sanders was politically active in the 1960s and was probably the best-known member of the rock group The Fugs.

GARY SNYDER. As a poet and in his person he has long been a spokesman for the natural world and the values that are associated with world cultures and traditions. In his twenties he was a practicing Zen Buddhist, and for many years he lived in Japan, where he developed a form of poetry based on the best and most enduring cultural and spiritual values of his native and adopted lands. Snyder's most famous work may be *Turtle Island* (1974), for which he won the Pulitzer Prize in 1975.

ANNE WALDMAN graduated from Bennington College in 1966, where she studied with Howard Nemerov and Bernard Malamud. Although she is considerably younger than the rest of the Beats, her style and her association with Allen Ginsberg as codirector of the Jack Kerouac School of Disembodied Poetics at the Naropa Institute in Colorado connect her with them. She is well known for having supervised the Poetry Project at St. Mark's Church in the Bowery, and has gained an international reputation as a reader-performer.

LEW WELCH spent his college years at Reed, in Portland, Oregon, where he roomed with Gary Snyder and Philip Whalen. Together they would later form the nucleus of the San Francisco Renaissance and become nationally known Beat poets. A slow, careful writer, his collected poems were published posthumously in 1979, eight years after he took a gun and disappeared into the Sierra Nevada Mountains.

PHILIP WHALEN has lived a private, semireclusive existence, managing to live on his own terms: without money, but with a wide circle of devoted friends. A prolific writer, his most widely circulated book is *On Bear's Head: Selected Poems* (1969). He has been for some years a practicing Zen Buddhist monk.

SUSAN BRIER, JEHANNE BIÉTRY-SALINGER CARLSON, and **HUGH ROMNEY** were poets of the moment who contributed to *Beatitude* and then returned to their private lives.

Books for Further Reading

Below are some books by and about the Beats. Volumes 16–17 of the *Dictionary of Literary Biography*, edited by Ann Charters, include a useful and convenient selection of Beat biographies. For a more complete listing of books and other materials by and about the Beats, you can look at Morgan Hickey's *Bohemian Register*. Although Hickey's book is hard to find, it's extensive and fairly up to date.

Allen, Donald M., ed. *The New American Poetry: 1945–1960*. New York: Grove, 1960.

Allen and George F. Butterick. *The Postmoderns: The New American Poetry Revisited*. New York: Grove, 1982.

Allen and Robert Creeley. *New American Story*. New York: Grove, 1965.

Allen and Warren Tallman, eds. *Poetics of the New American Poetry*. New York: Grove, 1974.

Bartlett, Lee, ed. *The Beats: Essays in Criticism*. Jefferson, NC: McFarland, 1981.

Beatitude Anthology. San Francisco: City Lights Books, 1960.

Beaulieu, Victor-Lévy. *Jack Kerouac: A Chicken-Essay*, translated by Sheila Fischman. Toronto: Coach House Press, 1975.

Berthoff, Warner. *A Literature Without Qualities: American Writing Since 1945*. Berkeley: University of California Press, 1979.

Charters, Ann, ed. *Dictionary of Literary Biography*. Vols. 16–17: The Beats: Literary Bohemians in Postwar America. Detroit: Gale Research Co., 1983.

Charters, Ann, ed. *The Portable Beat Reader*. New York: Viking Penguin, 1992.

Charters, Ann. *Scenes Along the Road: Photographs of the Desolation Angels, 1944–1960*. New York: Portents/Gotham Book Mart, 1970.

Charters, Samuel. *Some Poems/Poets: Studies in American Underground Poetry Since 1945*. Berkeley: Oyez, 1971.

Cook, Bruce. *The Beat Generation*. New York: Scribners, 1971.

Cook, Ralph T. *The City Lights Pocket Poets Series: A Descriptive Bibliography*. LaJolla, CA: McGilvery/Atticus Books, 1982.

di Prima, Diane. *Memoirs of a Beatnik*. New York: Olympia, 1969.

Ehrlich, J. W., ed. *Howl of the Censor: The Four Letter Word on Trial*. San Carlos, CA: Nourse, 1961.

Faas, Ekbert. *Towards a New American Poetics: Essays and Interviews*. Santa Barbara, CA: Black Sparrow Press, 1979.

Feldman, Gene and Max Gartenberg, eds. *The Beat Generation and the Angry Young Men*. New York: Citadel, 1958.

Ginsberg, Allen. *Collected Poems, 1947–1980*. New York: HarperCollins, 1988.

Hickey, Morgan. *The Bohemian Register: An Annotated Bibliography of the Beat Literary Movement*. Metuchen, NJ: Scarecrow Press, Inc., 1990.

Hipkiss, Robert A. *Jack Kerouac: Prophet of the New Romanticism*. Lawrence, KS: Regents Press of Kansas, 1976.

Johnson, Joyce. *Minor Characters*. Boston: Houghton Mifflin, 1983.

Jones, LeRoi, ed. *The Moderns: An Anthology of New Writing in America*. New York: Corinth, 1963.

Kherdian, David. *Six San Francisco Poets*. Fresno, CA: Giligia, 1969.

Knight, Arthur and Kit, eds. *Kerouac and the Beats: A Primary Source Book*. New York: Paragon House, 1988.

Kostelanetz, Richard. *Twenties in the Sixties*. Westport, CT: Greenwood Press, 1979.

Krim, Seymour, ed. *The Beats*. Greenwich, CT: Fawcett, 1960.

Lipton, Lawrence. *The Holy Barbarians*. New York: Messner, 1959.

Meltzer, David. comp. *The San Francisco Poets*. New York: Ballantine Books, 1971.

Parkinson, Thomas, ed. *A Casebook on the Beat*. New York: Crowell, 1961.

Peters, Robert. *The Great American Poetry Bake-Off*. Metuchen, NJ: Scarecrow Press, 1979.

Rigney, Francis J. and L. Douglas Smith. *The Real Bohemia: A Sociological and Psychological Study of the Beats*. New York: Basic Books, 1961.

Sanders, Ed. *Tales of Beatnik Glory*. New York: Stonehill, 1975.

Tytell, John. *Naked Angels: The Lives and Literature of the Beat Generation*. New York: Grove-Atlantic, 1986.

Wilentz, Elias, ed. *The Beat Scene*. New York: Corinth Books, 1960.